HELLO
FRESH

HELLO FRESH Unboxed

By **Kristin Bryan** & **Michelle Doll Olson**

Foreword by **Adam Kalikow, Managing Director HelloFresh US**

Photography by **Michael Piazza**

Salty Days Media Company LLC
98 Forest Avenue
Cohasset, MA 02025

First published in the United States by Salty Days Media Company LLC 2026

Library of Congress Cataloging-in-Publication Data
Name: Bryan, Kristin and Doll Olson, Michelle
Title: *HelloFresh Unboxed: 100+ Recipes for Real Life* /
Kristin Bryan, Michelle Doll Olson
Identifiers: LCCN 2026934527 (print) /
ISBN 979-8-9947213-7-7 (hardcover)

ISBN: 979-8-9947213-7-7

Distributed by Simon & Schuster Publishing Services
1 (800) 223-2336
Printed in China

Nutrition values are estimates only and may vary based on ingredient brands, portion sizes, preparation methods, and substitutions; optional ingredients are excluded. Values are calculated using standard ingredient databases and are intended for informational purposes only. This information should not be considered medical or nutritional advice. For specific dietary concerns, please consult a health-care professional.

Cover Photograph: Smoked Salmon Nicoise (page 155)

Publisher **Sara Domville**

Editorial Director **Kim Laidlaw**

Creative Director **Alexandra Zeigler**

Assistant Designer **Diana Heom**

Photographer **Michael Piazza**

Digital Tech/Photo Assistant **Dan Orlow**

Food Stylist **Joy Howard**

Food Stylist Assistants **Rachel Michel & Laura Sui**

Production Manager **Chris Hemesath**

Photo Agent **Michelle Bablitz**

WHY WE LOVE SALTY DAYS

In ancient Rome, salt was so valuable it served as currency—essential for preserving food and sustaining life. Today, Salty Days celebrates moments worth savoring: shared meals, stories, and connection around the table. That philosophy aligns with HelloFresh's belief that home cooking should be accessible, joyful, and human.

HelloFresh Unboxed, created with Salty Days Media, brings that vision to life—highlighting fresh ingredients, confident cooking, and the people behind the meals reaching millions each week. Founded by Publisher Sara Domville, Salty Days Media partners with leading brands to create meaningful stories that inspire connection, creativity, and flavor.

For more information, contact Sara Domville at **saradomville@saltydays.com**.

1

2

3

4

5

6

7

8

Welcome

At HelloFresh, we believe deeply in the power of home cooking. When we talk about what makes HelloFresh special, it always comes back to one simple idea: the joy of cooking made easy. Every week, millions of people open one of our boxes, pull out fresh ingredients, and create something delicious at home. That moment, when dinner hits the table and everyone gathers around, is what drives us. It's what connects us not only as a company but also as cooks, parents, partners, and friends.

Cooking at home has never been about perfection. It's about connection. And we believe convenience doesn't have to come at the expense of creativity. In fact, the right kind of convenience can unlock it. When the planning, shopping, and guesswork are simplified, what's left is the part that really matters: the joy of cooking itself. The smell of garlic in a warm pan. The chatter in the kitchen. The first bite that makes you pause and say, "Wow, that's really good."

This cookbook is a celebration of home cooking. In these pages, you'll find recipes from the people who bring HelloFresh to life, like our employees, recipe developers, and ingredient vendors. These are dishes that have been cooked, shared, and loved in kitchens all over the country. Each one tells a story, whether it's a family favorite passed down through generations or a weeknight win discovered on a busy Tuesday.

Our hope is that these recipes inspire you to keep cooking, and to share those moments with the people around you. Because when we cook together, we're not just feeding ourselves. We're building memories, one meal at a time.

So grab your apron, turn up your favorite playlist, and make something delicious. From all of us at HelloFresh, thank you for inviting us into your kitchen. We're honored to cook with you.

Adam Kalikow

Adam Kalikow
Managing Director, HelloFresh US

About HelloFresh

Our Story

HelloFresh began with a simple idea: to help people fall in love with cooking at home again. In 2011, a small team started packing up fresh ingredients and simple recipe cards, believing that everyone should be able to cook a delicious homemade meal without the stress of planning or shopping. What started as a handful of boxes has grown into a global community of home cooks, with HelloFresh now delivering millions of meals each week across eighteen countries.

More Than Convenience

Our mission has always been about more than convenience. It's about connection too. We believe food has the power to bring people together and create meaningful moments at the table. Whether it's a weeknight dinner after a long day or a new recipe that sparks a shared memory, our goal is to make those moments easier to create and more joyful to experience.

How We Cook

We cook the way people love to eat: seasonally, simply, and with balance in mind. Each recipe starts with ingredients at their peak. Our Culinary Team works closely with farmers and suppliers to bring the best of each season into your kitchen, because good meals start long before they reach your plate. From sourcing to portioning, we're always looking for ways to make cooking at home easier without sacrificing flavor or quality. Every recipe is tested until it feels just right—whether it's a comfort food favorite or a chance to try a new skill—so your dish looks beautiful, tastes even better, and works in real life.

For Every Table

Cooking is for everyone, and our recipes reflect that. We offer options for every lifestyle and skill level, whether you're vegetarian, looking for calorie-smart meals, or teaching your kids to stir their first sauce. Dinner is more than a meal. It's a moment to learn, to share, and to connect. We see every recipe as an invitation to slow down, gather around the table, and rediscover what dinner can mean.

MEALS WITH MEANING

Across the United States, 48 million people, including 14 million children* face food insecurity—meaning they don't always have reliable access to the food they need to live healthy, fulfilling lives. As a meal kit company built around fresh ingredients and home cooking, that reality is impossible for us to ignore. It's why we're committed to finding meaningful ways to make wholesome food more accessible across the country.

Meals with Meaning was launched in 2020 to help address rising food insecurity. Through the program, we work closely with nonprofit partners in communities near our distribution centers to provide free HelloFresh meal kits—complete with fresh ingredients and easy-to-follow-recipe cards—so individuals and families can come together to prepare nourishing meals at home. To date, Meals with Meaning has delivered more than 10 million meals to those facing food insecurity across the U.S.

**FeedingAmerica.org*

Ingredients with Integrity

We believe the story of every great meal begins long before it reaches your kitchen. It starts in the soil, on the sea, and with the hands of the people who grow, harvest, and craft the ingredients we use.

That's why we work with suppliers who share our values: partners who honor the land, respect their workers, and commit to practices that protect the future of food. When ingredients are raised with care, they hold a kind of quiet magic, deeper flavor, brighter color, and natural richness.

Responsibly sourced ingredients simply taste better. They're the vegetables picked at peak ripeness, the herbs grown without shortcuts, and the proteins that collectively ensure the well-being of our planet and society. These choices don't just elevate a recipe; they honor the ecosystems and communities behind every bite. When you cook with integrity, from the olive oil in your skillet to the vegetables on your cutting board, you can taste the difference in every bite.

But this commitment isn't about perfection or exclusivity. It's about progress, transparency, and a belief that delicious food and responsible sourcing should go hand in hand. As you explore the recipes in this cookbook, you'll find meals that celebrate life, culture, memories, flavors, and heartfelt cooking from the HelloFresh team members who care about what's on your plate.

FUN FAMILY IDEA

Start a "waste log" for one week. Put a note on the fridge and have everyone write down every time food scraps or spoiled food is thrown away (not composted). Review the log at the end of the week and brainstorm how to eliminate those items next time!

Sustainability at HelloFresh

At HelloFresh, we think about sustainability the same way we think about cooking: with curiosity, intention, and a whole lot of care. Every recipe in this book, every ingredient, every box is shaped by a belief that great food should nourish people and protect the planet. Here's how we bring that belief to life across our kitchens, communities, and supply chains.

A Lighter Footprint, One Box at a Time

We've been doing the behind-the-scenes work to make each meal kit gentler on the planet.

- Today, 100 percent of the electricity we use in our facilities comes from renewable sources.
- By working with domestic suppliers where and when we can, and buying directly from producers, we shorten the distance ingredients travel, cutting emissions and delivering fresher food.
- A recent Life Cycle Assessment found that a HelloFresh meal kit has a 31 percent lower carbon footprint than the same meal from the supermarket.
- And because our ingredients arrive preportioned and our recipes are intentionally designed, this reduces food waste related to making dinner by at least 38 percent.

We work with suppliers who share our values because responsibly sourced ingredients simply taste better. All of our seafood follows Monterey Bay Aquarium Seafood Watch recommendations or comes from producers certified by independent programs, like the Marine Stewardship Council, Aquaculture Stewardship Council, Best Aquaculture Practices, or GLOBALG.A.P. These partnerships ensure quality, traceability, and care for the ecosystems that sustain us.

Food That Never Goes to Waste

We believe surplus food should feed people, not landfills. Since 2019, we've donated 43.5 million pounds of unsold ingredients—equivalent to thirty-three million meals—to charities across the country. These donations help reduce waste while supporting communities where nutritious fresh food is too often out of reach.

PANTRY PARTNER SPOTLIGHT: ROLAND FOODS

Roland Foods has been providing home cooks with global pantry staples since the 1930s. Founded in France and later rooted in the United States, the company has always focused on sourcing interesting, high-quality ingredients from producers around the world, many of whom the company has worked with for decades.

If you cook with HelloFresh regularly, you've probably tasted its products without even realizing it. For example, Roland Foods' toasted sesame oil, hoisin sauce, and vegan oyster sauce are dependable favorites for adding depth and character to quick weeknight cooking, such as the recipe for Mushroom Banh Mi on page 208.

Think of Roland Foods and its line of global pantry items as an extra helper in the kitchen that makes recipes like this riff on the popular Vietnamese sandwich easy to pull off at home.

YELLOW CARROTS
PURPLE CARROTS
BEETS
GOLDEN BEETS
FRESH

PANTRY PARTNER SPOTLIGHT: COLAVITA

In the hilltop village of Sant'Elia a Pianisi in Italy's Molise region, two humble family trades took root generations ago, one pressing olives into vibrant extra-virgin olive oil, the other milling durum wheat into fresh pasta for the local community. These were the livelihoods of the Colavita family, craftspeople whose dedication to quality was passed down like an heirloom.

Today, those small family operations have grown into the globally trusted Colavita brand, still guided by the same family and the same commitment to authenticity. With facilities in Molise, in Pomezia in Italy's Lazio region, and in US locations in New Jersey and California, Colavita has shared Italian ingredients with the world since 1979. "Quality and tradition [are] very important to us and will always continue to be," says Giovanni Colavita, CEO of Colavita USA.

That devotion shows in every product. Olives are harvested at peak ripeness and pressed immediately, and pasta is made from 100 percent durum wheat and the pristine spring water of Molise. Each item is rigorously tested to ensure only the best reaches your kitchen.

Colavita also embraces the spirit of the Italian table, where food nourishes connection and well-being, and pairs that with a deep commitment to community and sustainability, from solar-powered facilities to charitable initiatives focused on food security and food education.

A Table Big Enough for Everyone

Food is connection, and everyone deserves a seat at the table. Through our social impact programs, we help meet immediate needs while building long-term community resilience.

Meals with Meaning

We provide eight thousand free meal kits every week, supporting families in Dallas–Fort Worth, Newark, New York City, Phoenix, and beyond. To date, this program has delivered more than ten million meals to households facing food insecurity.

LimeAid

Neighbors nominate neighbors. Families receive twelve free weeks of meals when they need it most. Nearly five hundred families across the country have been supported through this simple but powerful act of community care.

No Kid Hungry

With one in five children in the United States experiencing food insecurity, our partnership with No Kid Hungry helps ensure kids have access to three meals a day, 365 days a year. From fundraising efforts to community events to research-backed solutions, we're committed to helping end childhood hunger.

Inside The HelloFresh Test Kitchen

Just around the corner from Wall Street in New York—past elevators, office desks, and the predictable rhythm of corporate life—lies a space that feels entirely different. Here, the lights flick on before sunrise, the ovens warm up like old friends, and the air fills with the sound of chopping, simmering, and the kind of easy laughter that comes from a collaborative team that moves like a well-oiled machine. It's here, in this bright, energetic kitchen, that every HelloFresh meal begins.

A Day in the Test Kitchen

Most mornings, the first one in is Kenia, our kitchen porter. She moves through the space with the assurance of someone who knows every dial on the ovens and every spice in the pantry by heart. As she starts the day, the chef/recipe developers arrive with laptops under their arms, aprons tied loosely, and notebooks brimming with ideas. Coffee brews, produce is unpacked, and mise en place begins to gather across the long stainless-steel counters. It may look like organized chaos from the outside, but every person here knows exactly why they've come: to create meals that make dinnertime feel possible, joyful, and delicious for families everywhere.

On any given day, the team tastes upward of sixteen dishes—everything from twenty-minute weeknight winners to globally inspired meals and vegetarian favorites. Each recipe represents a carefully crafted idea: something comforting, something adventurous, something fresh, or something that simply solves the 6:00 p.m. "What's for dinner?" dilemma. But before a recipe appears on the HelloFresh menu or lands in a customer's box, it has to pass a demanding series of tests. It must be delicious, easy to follow, nutritionally balanced, cost-effective, and achievable for home cooks of all skill levels.

"We're not just chefs—we're problem solvers, teachers, and dinner companions from afar."

—CHRISTINA BOATENG, RECIPE DEVELOPER

"We read every customer comment. Every single one. Your feedback shapes what we create next."

—AVRAM SALZMANN, RECIPE DEVELOPER

3 Sisters

Who's in the Kitchen?

The HelloFresh Culinary Team brings together an extraordinary range of backgrounds: fine-dining chefs, private chefs, food scientists, cookbook authors, restaurant owners, and even a former salmon fisherman. Some grew up in bustling multigenerational kitchens, others trained in formal culinary programs, and many have lived and cooked around the globe. What they share is a belief that home cooking matters—and that great home cooking starts long before the ingredients reach your doorstep.

Alongside the chefs are nutritionists who review recipes for balance and clarity, product specialists who find us the best most sustainable ingredients, food stylists who refine the presentation so the dish looks as good as it tastes, and culinary strategists, who make sure they have our finger on the pulse of what you want to eat.

The Recipe Development Process

A new recipe begins with inspiration: a seasonal ingredient that deserves the spotlight, a trend that's catching fire on social media, a classic cuisine reimagined in a modern, approachable way. Developers create several versions of a concept, adjusting flavor profiles, simplifying steps, or rethinking techniques to make sure the recipe feels fun and rewarding rather than intimidating.

In the testing phase, every measurement is scrutinized, every technique refined, and every flavor balanced. Recipes are tested fresh, made again with preportioned ingredients, and checked for consistency. Nothing moves forward until multiple chefs agree it works.

Testing for Togetherness

HelloFresh recipes are designed not only for efficiency but also for connection. Developers think carefully about how families cook together—how a child might help whisk a sauce, how a busy parent might divide tasks, how ingredients can be prepped in parallel to save time. They favor steps that build confidence: seasoning, searing, balancing acid, and introducing flavor boosters that become tools for future home cooking.

When a recipe encourages teamwork—like build-your-own tacos, customizable bowls, or shared pasta dishes—it gets extra consideration. These meals aren't just about feeding people; they're about bringing them together.

"The kitchen is a laboratory, yes. But it's also a place of joy. We want that joy to reach your table."

—MARA CASSIDY, CULINARY PRODUCT STRATEGY

"Good instructions matter as much as good flavor. Our job is to make you feel confident, not overwhelmed."

—JUDSON KNIFFEN, EDITOR

Where Innovation Happens

Innovation is central to the HelloFresh Test Kitchen. Developers analyze customer ratings from our Insights team, trends, emerging cuisines, global flavors, and feedback from millions of US households. They study the nuances of regional tastes—spicy in the Southwest, creamy in the Midwest, vegetable-forward on the West Coast. If customers say a dish needs more crunch or more sauce, it changes. If weeknight cooks ask for more one-pan meals, the team responds.

Sometimes inspiration comes from outside the menu altogether: the foods developers grew up eating, the dishes they crave after long days, the holiday recipes tied to memory and identity. These "outside the box" creations often become the seeds of future menu favorites—and they form the heart of this cookbook.

Why This Cookbook?

The *HelloFresh Unboxed* cookbook opens the doors of the Test Kitchen wider than ever before. It's a collection of recipes that the team cooks at home—comfort dishes, celebration meals, shortcuts, memories. These are the recipes that inspire our menus rather than appear on them, shaped by the same thoughtful process but rooted in personal stories.

The book is an invitation to cook with the same curiosity, creativity, rigor, and joy that fill the HelloFresh Test Kitchen every day. And above all, it's a celebration of the people who dedicate their days to making sure your nights feel a little easier.

Cooking The HelloFresh Way

If there's one thing years in kitchens, professional and home alike, have taught us, it's that cooking for real families is beautifully unpredictable. Dinner unfolds in the middle of life. The dog sneaks in for crumbs. Kids negotiate vegetables. Laundry hums in the background. It doesn't need to be perfect to be meaningful. It doesn't need to be fancy to feel special. But it does need to feel easy, and, ideally, joyful.

That belief sits at the center of everything we create at HelloFresh. Whether we're developing a Tuesday-night skillet for millions of households or crafting recipes for this cookbook, we're thinking about how real people cook in real kitchens. Our job is to make dinner feel less like an obligation and more like a moment you can enjoy.

Cooking the HelloFresh way means things are figured out in advance—the ingredients, timing, technique—so you can focus on what matters. We think of it as achievable excellence. Whole foods, smart shortcuts, and clear instructions that build confidence every time you cook. Dinner is solved, but more importantly, dinner is shared. It's a pause in the day, a ritual, and a chance to reconnect.

Cook with Confidence

You don't need a restaurant pantry or culinary-school training to cook well at home. What you need is confidence and the understanding that small, thoughtful choices add up to better food. Every HelloFresh recipe is built on three simple pillars:

1. Simplicity

Good food doesn't require twenty ingredients. In fact, a few quality ingredients often make a dish shine. Think of Italian cooking at its best: ripe tomatoes, fragrant basil, a drizzle of great olive oil. Nothing unnecessary. Just what's fresh and true. We write recipes as building blocks with clear steps, no guesswork, and no mystery. The groceries are already there, and the techniques are approachable. The cleanup is manageable. Simplicity isn't cutting corners. It's focusing on what actually matters.

2. Timing & Balance

Home cooking has a rhythm. Season early. Sear with intention. Pull food off the heat before it goes too far. If something tastes flat, it's usually missing salt or contrast—a squeeze of fresh lemon juice, a splash of vinegar, a pinch of red pepper flakes. We look for balance in every dish, which means developing flavors that are rich but with a touch of brightness, carry heat along with sweetness, and pair crisp edges with creamy centers. That contrast is what makes food memorable.

3. Make It Yours

Recipes aren't rules. They're invitations! Swap what you have. Use your freezer as your ally. Taste as you go. The best home cooks aren't rigid. They're responsive, curious, and playful.

This cookbook is full of opportunities to riff, adjust, and make each dish your own. That's where confidence really grows.

Sustainability Starts at Home

Sustainability isn't only about big initiatives. It lives in small kitchen habits that reduce waste, save money, and make weeknights easier. These are small steps with big impact.

Here are a few every-day rituals we swear by:

- Store herbs like flowers. Trim the stems, place in water, and refrigerate.
- Freeze leftover pesto, sauces, or chopped herbs in ice-cube trays.
- Treat your freezer like a pantry. Ginger, bread, cheese, broth, and grains all freeze beautifully.
- Save Parmesan rinds. They turn simple soups into something extraordinary.

Cooking as Connection

For us, cooking isn't just a task. It's a form of care—a moment in the day when things slow down just enough to feel like living. Whether you're handing a child a wooden spoon, catching up with a partner, or cooking just for yourself, dinner is a chance to show up.

The people you cook for won't remember whether your onions were perfectly diced. They'll remember being at the table with you. If a HelloFresh meal kit helps you get dinner on the table with more ease, use it. If a slow weekend project like homemade tomato sauce brings you joy, make it. And if this cookbook becomes a trusted companion in your kitchen, easing your weeknights and inspiring new favorites, then we've done our job.

Domino
POWDERED SUGAR
CRAFTED by EXPERTS
Domino
Since 1901

HELLO
FRESH

How To Use This Book

The *HelloFresh Unboxed* cookbook is more than a collection of recipes. It's a celebration of home cooking, creativity, and connection. Whether you've been cooking with HelloFresh for years or you're discovering us for the first time, this book is designed to inspire you to bring fresh ideas and easy confidence to every meal.

Inside, you'll find more than one hundred recipes that reflect the heart of HelloFresh—dishes created, tested, and loved by the chefs and innovators in our Test Kitchen, as well as a handful from our employees, their families, and ingredient vendors. Each chapter offers a mix of familiar favorites and new discoveries, from quick weeknight dinners to inspired weekend meals and global flavors that bring the world to your table.

Every recipe includes clear step-by-step instructions, cooking tips, and serving suggestions designed to make your time in the kitchen both effortless and enjoyable. You'll also find practical notes about ingredient swaps and ways to make each dish your own—just like our HelloFresh recipe cards but with even more depth, story, and flavor.

As you cook through these pages, take a moment to meet the incredible team behind the recipes. Throughout the book, you'll find spotlights on our Test Kitchen chefs and recipe developers—the creative minds who dream up the meals that arrive at your doorstep each week. They'll share their favorite ingredients, their go-to techniques, and the simple joy of cooking with fresh food.

We also invite you to use this book as a companion to your HelloFresh box. Explore a new recipe on nights when you're not cooking from a kit, or use the stories and tips to inspire your own kitchen experiments. You might even rediscover a favorite recipe from a past box, now with added chef insights and clever ways to customize it for your family.

Most of all, we hope this book brings you joy in the process, from choosing ingredients to that first delicious bite. Cooking at home should feel like an adventure, not a chore. So turn the pages, roll up your sleeves, and cook a little "outside the box."

From our kitchen to yours, happy cooking and thank you for being part of the HelloFresh family.

1 Mix & Match

Protein

+

Sauce

+

Side Dish

Think of this chapter as your ultimate kitchen playbook: a guide to cooking confidently, creatively, and deliciously with whatever you have on hand. The HelloFresh Test Kitchen designed these recipes to help you build incredible meals from a handful of versatile components: proteins, sauces, and sides that can be mixed and matched into endless combinations.

We know life doesn't always follow a recipe card. Some nights you have time for a full dinner spread; other nights you just want something fast, fresh, and flavorful. This chapter gives you both: a flexible toolkit of tested recipes and trusted flavor pairings that make home cooking easy and exciting.

Start by choosing your **protein**. Whether it's seared tofu, pan-roasted chicken, roasted pork tenderloin, grilled flank steak or shrimp kebabs, or baked salmon fillets, every option has been perfected for flavor, texture, and simplicity. These are your building blocks—reliable, go-to recipes you can return to week after week.

Next, choose your **sauce**, where the real personality shines. If you love the classics, try our signature basil pesto or tangy teriyaki. If you're feeling adventurous, switch things up with arugula pesto or vibrant Vietnamese nước chấm. To bring restaurant-style elegance to your table, spoon over creamy mustard sauce, salsa verde, lemon miso butter, or a rich mushroom herb sauce.

Round out your plate with your favorite **side dish**. Buttery mashed potatoes, mashed parsnips, or butternut squash purée bring cozy comfort, while garlicky green rice, roasted vegetables, or stir-fried greens keep things light, colorful, and balanced. Each side is designed to complement any protein and sauce, so no matter what's in your pantry, fridge, or freezer, you'll have something that works beautifully together.

The magic of mix and match is that there's no wrong answer—only delicious possibilities. A million combinations await, ready to fit your cravings, schedule, and family's tastes. Open your fridge, flip through these pages, and let your mood lead the menu. Dinner, your way: fresh, fast, and full of flavor.

Some of Our Favorite Recipe Combinations

Proteins

Roast Pork Tenderloin

MAKES 4 SERVINGS

1 pork tenderloin (1½ lb/680 g)

Kosher salt and freshly ground pepper

2 Tbsp olive or vegetable oil

PAN SAUCE (OPTIONAL)

¼ cup (60 ml) heavy cream

¼ cup (60 ml) dry white wine or apple cider

1 tsp Dijon mustard

Kosher salt and freshly ground pepper

Preheat the oven to 400°F (200°C). Pat the tenderloin dry with paper towels. Season with salt and pepper.

To brown the tenderloin, preheat a large ovenproof skillet over medium-high heat, then add the oil. When the oil is hot, add the tenderloin and sear, turning until golden brown on all sides, 6 to 9 minutes.

To roast the tenderloin, transfer the skillet to the oven. Roast until an instant-read thermometer inserted into the thickest part registers 140° to 145°F (60° to 63°C) for a slightly pink center, 12 to 18 minutes. Transfer the pork to a cutting board, tent with aluminum foil, and let rest for 5 to 10 minutes.

To make the pan sauce, if using, return the skillet to the stovetop over medium heat. Add the cream and wine and stir together, scraping up any browned bits from the pan bottom. Stir in the mustard, bring to a simmer, and cook, stirring, until slightly reduced, 3 to 5 minutes. Season with salt and pepper.

To serve, slice the pork into medallions. Drizzle with the pan sauce, if using.

Nutrition Values (per serving): Energy (kJ) ~1381 kJ, Calories ~330 kcal, Fat ~18 g, Saturated Fat ~6 g, Carbohydrate ~2 g, Sugar ~1 g, Dietary Fiber 0 g, Protein ~32 g, Cholesterol ~105 mg, Sodium ~450 mg

Grilled Flank Steak

MAKES 4 TO 6 SERVINGS

⅓ cup (80 ml) dry red wine

¼ cup (60 ml) soy sauce

4 garlic cloves, minced

1 Tbsp light brown sugar

1 flank steak (about 1½ lb/680 g), trimmed of silverskin

To marinate the steak, in a small bowl, whisk together the wine, soy sauce, garlic, and sugar until the sugar dissolves. Lay the steak flat in a medium baking dish, pour the marinade over the top, then turn the steak to coat evenly. Cover and refrigerate for at least 30 minutes or up to overnight. Let the steak sit at room temperature for about 30 minutes before cooking.

Prepare a charcoal or gas grill for direct cooking over medium-high heat (450°F/230°C). When the grill is ready, brush the grill grates clean. Alternatively, preheat a stovetop grill pan large enough to accommodate the steak over medium-high heat.

To grill the steak, remove it from the marinade, letting any excess marinade drip off. Place the steak on the grill grates directly over the fire, close the lid, and grill the steak, turning once halfway through cooking, until done to your liking, about 10 minutes total for medium-rare. Or place the steak on the preheated grill pan and grill, turning once halfway through cooking, following the same timing. Transfer the steak to a cutting board and let rest for 5 to 10 minutes.

To serve, cut the steak across the grain into slices ¼ inch (6 mm) thick.

Nutrition Values (per serving for 6 servings): Energy (kJ) ~1297 kJ, Calories ~310 kcal, Fat ~18 g, Saturated Fat ~7 g, Carbohydrate ~4 g, Sugar ~3 g, Dietary Fiber 0 g, Protein ~28 g, Cholesterol ~80 mg, Sodium ~750 mg

Pan-Roasted Chicken Thighs

MAKES 4 SERVINGS

4 large bone-in, skin-on chicken thighs (about 1½ lb/680 g)

Kosher salt and freshly ground pepper

To season the chicken, pat the thighs dry with paper towels. Season generously all over with salt and pepper, including under the skin.

To crisp the skin, arrange the chicken thighs, skin-side down, in a single layer in a large cast-iron skillet and place over medium-high heat (no oil is needed; the fat of the chicken skin will render). Sear until the skin releases easily from the skillet and is crisp and deep golden brown, 6 to 8 minutes.

To finish cooking, turn the thighs and sear the flesh side until nicely browned, about 5 minutes. Turn down the heat to medium-low, cover the pan, and cook until an instant-read thermometer inserted into the thickest part of a thigh not touching bone registers 165°F (74°C), 10 to 12 minutes. Transfer to a plate and let rest for 5 minutes before serving.

Nutrition Values (per serving): Energy (kJ) ~1213 kJ, Calories ~290 kcal, Fat ~20 g, Saturated Fat ~6 g, Carbohydrate 0 g, Sugar 0 g, Dietary Fiber 0 g, Protein ~24 g, Cholesterol ~115 mg, Sodium ~400 mg (depends on salt used)

Grilled Chicken Breasts

MAKES 4 SERVINGS

1½ lb (680 g) boneless, skinless chicken breasts

Kosher salt and freshly ground pepper

Extra virgin olive oil, for drizzling

To prep the chicken, lay a chicken breast on a cutting board. Using the flat side of a meat mallet (or the bottom of a small, heavy skillet), gently pound the chicken to an even thickness of about ¾ inch (2 cm). Transfer to a large plate. Repeat with the remaining chicken breasts and add to the plate. Season the breasts generously all over with salt and pepper, then drizzle with oil, coating them lightly on both sides.

Prepare a charcoal or gas grill for direct cooking over medium-high heat (450°F/230°C). When the grill is ready, brush the grill grates clean. Alternatively, preheat a stovetop grill pan large enough to accommodate the chicken breasts over medium-high heat.

To grill the chicken, place on the grill grates directly over the fire and grill, turning once or twice, until nicely etched with grill marks and cooked through but still juicy, 8 to 11 minutes total. Or place the chicken on the preheated grill pan and grill, turning once or twice, following the same timing. Transfer to a plate and let rest for at least 5 minutes. Serve warm or or let cool to room temperature.

Nutrition Values (per serving): Energy (kJ) 1200 kJ, Calories 285 kcal, Fat 7 g ,Saturated Fat 1.5 g, Carbohydrate 0 g, Sugar 0 g, Dietary Fiber 0 g, Protein 45 g, Cholesterol 135 mg, Sodium 170mg

Grilled Shrimp Kebabs

MAKES 4 SERVINGS

16 to 20 jumbo shrimp, peeled and deveined

3 Tbsp extra virgin olive oil

3 garlic cloves, minced

Kosher salt and freshly ground pepper

½ lemon

Soak 4 long bamboo skewers in cold water to cover for 30 minutes.

Prepare a charcoal or gas grill for direct cooking over medium heat (350° to 400°F/175° to 200°C). When the grill is ready, brush the grill grates clean.

While the grill heats, prep the shrimp. In a medium bowl, combine the shrimp, oil, and garlic and turn to coat the shrimp evenly. Thread the shrimp onto the soaked skewers, piercing each shrimp twice, once through the tail end and once through the thickest part near the head end (this keeps the shrimp flat when you turn the skewers on the grill). Season the shrimp on both sides with salt and pepper.

To grill the shrimp, arrange the skewers on the grill grates directly over the fire. Grill, turning as needed, until the shrimp are opaque throughout, about 6 minutes.

To serve, transfer the shrimp to a platter and squeeze the juice from the lemon half over the top.

Nutrition Values (per serving): Energy (kJ) ~753 kJ, Calories ~180 kcal, Fat ~8 g, Saturated Fat ~1 g, Carbohydrate ~1 g, Sugar ~0 g, Dietary Fiber 0 g, Protein ~24 g, Cholesterol ~180 mg, Sodium ~500 mg (mostly from shrimp and added salt)

Panfried Halibut

MAKES 4 SERVINGS

4 skinless halibut or other white fish fillets, such as cod, haddock, or snapper (about 6 oz/170 g each), pin bones removed

Kosher salt and freshly ground pepper

2 Tbsp olive oil

2 Tbsp unsalted butter or compound butter (pages 47 to 48)

To prep the fish, pat the fillets dry with paper towels. This step is key to creating a golden, crisp crust. Season all over with salt and pepper.

To sear the fillets, in a large nonstick or stainless-steel skillet over medium-high heat, warm the oil. When the oil is shimmering, add the fillets, skinned-side up and in a single layer, and cook without moving until the bottom is golden and the fish releases easily from the pan, 3 to 4 minutes.

Turn down the heat to medium, add the butter, and gently flip the fillets. Spoon the melted butter over the top of the fillets as they finish cooking, 2 to 3 minutes. The fish is ready when it is just cooked through (barely opaque and still moist) and flakes easily with a fork. Transfer to a platter or plates and serve at once.

Cook's Notes

For a hint of brightness, finish the fillets with a squeeze of fresh lemon juice or a splash of white wine.

Nutrition Values (per serving): Energy (kJ) ~1172 kJ, Calories ~280 kcal, Fat ~16 g, Saturated Fat ~6 g, Carbohydrate 0 g, Sugar 0 g, Dietary Fiber 0 g, Protein ~28 g, Cholesterol ~75 mg, Sodium ~350 mg (depends on salt used)

Baked Salmon Fillets

MAKES 4 SERVINGS

4 salmon, cod, halibut, or haddock fillets (6 to 8 oz/170 to 225 g each), preferably skinless, pin bones removed

4 Tbsp (55 g) unsalted butter, compound butter (pages 47 to 48), or extra virgin olive oil

Kosher salt and freshly ground pepper

1 lemon, thinly sliced into rounds

Preheat the oven to 350°F (175°C). Cut four pieces of parchment paper or aluminum foil, each about 12 inches (30 cm) square (big enough to wrap each fillet securely).

To assemble each packet, place a salmon fillet vertically in the center of a piece of parchment or foil. Top with 1 Tbsp of the butter and season with salt and pepper. Lay a lemon slice on top. Lift the two longer sides of the parchment or foil to meet in the middle above the fillet. Tightly roll the parchment or foil down to meet the fish, then crimp and roll the ends, tucking them underneath the packet to seal securely. Transfer the packets to a large sheet pan.

Bake the packets until the fish is just cooked through, about 10 minutes for a thinner fillet or 15 minutes for a thicker fillet.

To check for doneness, carefully open one packet and test the fish with the tip of a knife. It should be just cooked through (barely opaque and still moist) and flake easily. Avoid overcooking.

To serve, transfer each packet to a dinner plate and open at the table.

Nutrition Values (per serving): Energy (kJ) ~1464 kJ, Calories ~350 kcal, Fat ~22 g, Saturated Fat ~7 g, Carbohydrate 0 g, Sugar 0 g, Dietary Fiber 0 g, Protein ~34 g, Cholesterol ~95 mg, Sodium ~400 mg (depends on salt used)

Seared Tofu

MAKES 4 SERVINGS

1 (14- to 16-oz/400- to 450-g) block firm tofu, drained

Kosher salt, if not using marinade

1 to 2 Tbsp vegetable oil

MARINADE (OPTIONAL)

2 Tbsp soy sauce or tamari

1 Tbsp rice vinegar

2 tsp toasted sesame oil

½ tsp ground white pepper

1 tsp peeled and finely grated fresh ginger

Pat the tofu block dry with paper towels, then wrap it in a kitchen towel or paper towels and place on a small sheet pan. Set a heavy weight, such as a cast-iron skillet, on top for 15 to 20 minutes to remove excess moisture. Unwrap the tofu and cut into planks ½ inch (12 mm) thick or into ½-inch (12-mm) cubes. If not using marinade, season the tofu all over with salt.

To marinate the tofu (optional), in a shallow dish, whisk together the marinade ingredients. Add the tofu. Marinate for at least 15 minutes or for up to 1 hour. Remove it from the marinade, then gently pat the pieces with paper towels to remove excess moisture.

To cook the tofu, in a large nonstick or stainless-steel skillet over medium-high heat, add the vegetable oil. When the oil is shimmering, add the tofu pieces in a single layer and cook, turning once, until crisp and golden brown on both sides, 6 to 8 minutes.

Transfer the tofu to a platter or shallow bowl and serve immediately.

Nutrition Values (per serving): Energy (kJ) ~628 kJ, Calories ~150 kcal, Fat ~10 g, Saturated Fat ~1.5 g, Carbohydrate ~4 g, Sugar ~1 g, Dietary Fiber ~1 g, Protein ~10 g, Cholesterol 0 mg (tofu is plant-based), Sodium ~300 mg (higher if using soy sauce marinade)

Sauces

Classic Basil Pesto

MAKES ABOUT 1 CUP (240 G)

2 cups (24 g) lightly packed fresh basil leaves

½ cup (15 g) grated Parmesan or pecorino cheese

¼ cup (30 g) pine nuts

1 garlic clove, chopped

Kosher salt and freshly ground pepper

½ cup (120 ml) extra virgin olive oil

To make the pesto, a food processor, combine the basil, cheese, pine nuts, garlic, and a pinch each of salt and pepper. Pulse a few times until the ingredients are all roughly chopped and mixed.

With the motor running, slowly drizzle in the oil until it is fully incorporated and a moderately thick, slightly textured paste has formed. As you add the oil, stop the machine and scrape down the sides of the bowl.

Taste and adjust the seasoning with salt or pepper if needed. Use the pesto right away or transfer to an airtight container, top with a thin layer of oil to slow discoloration, and refrigerate for up to 1 week.

Cook's Notes

For arugula-walnut pesto, substitute baby arugula for the basil leaves, use pecorino rather than Parmesan, and swap in lightly toasted chopped walnuts for the pine nuts, then proceed as directed. Add a squeeze of fresh lemon juice at the end.

Nutrition Values (per 2-Tbsp serving): Energy (kJ) ~795 kJ, Calories ~190 kcal, Fat ~19 g, Saturated Fat ~3 g, Carbohydrate ~2 g, Sugar ~0 g, Dietary Fiber ~1 g, Protein ~2 g, Cholesterol ~5 mg, Sodium ~150 mg

Kale Pesto

MAKES ABOUT 1 CUP (240 G)

½ cup (120 ml) extra virgin olive oil

3 oz (85 g) dinosaur kale leaves, stemmed and chopped

½ cup (6 g) lightly packed fresh basil leaves

1 cup (30 g) grated pecorino or Parmesan cheese

⅓ cup (40 g) pine nuts or chopped walnuts

Kosher salt and freshly ground pepper

To make the pesto, add the oil to a food processor, followed by the kale, basil, cheese, nuts, salt, and pepper. Process, stopping the machine and scraping down the sides of the bowl as needed, until the mixture is finely chopped and well mixed.

Taste and adjust the seasoning with salt or pepper if needed. Use the pesto right away or transfer to an airtight container, top with a thin layer of oil to slow discoloration, and refrigerate for up to 3 days.

Cook's Notes

Dark green, bumpy-leaved dinosaur kale is also known as Tuscan or lacinato kale and cavolo nero.

For a quick dinner, toss either pesto with freshly cooked pasta, such as trofie or fusilli, or gnocchi. Before mixing the pesto with the pasta or gnocchi, stir a spoonful or two of the warm pasta water into the pesto to create a silkier, creamier coating consistency.

Nutrition Values (per 2-Tbsp serving): Energy (kJ) ~837 kJ, Calories ~200 kcal, Fat ~20 g, Saturated Fat ~4 g, Carbohydrate ~2 g, Sugar ~0 g, Dietary Fiber ~1 g, Protein ~3 g, Cholesterol ~7 mg, Sodium ~160 mg

Teriyaki Sauce

MAKES ABOUT ¾ CUP (175 ML)

¼ cup (60 ml) soy sauce or tamari
¼ cup (60 ml) mirin
2 Tbsp sake
2 Tbsp peeled and finely grated apple or pear
1 garlic clove, minced
1 tsp peeled and finely grated fresh ginger
1 tsp cornstarch mixed with 1 Tbsp cold water (optional)

To make the sauce, in a small saucepan over medium heat, whisk together the soy sauce, mirin, sake, apple, garlic, and ginger. Bring to a gentle boil, then turn down the heat to low and simmer, stirring occasionally, until slightly reduced and fragrant, 5 to 6 minutes.

For a glossy, clingy sauce, briefly stir the cornstarch mixture to recombine, then add to the pan and simmer, stirring, until the sauce coats the back of a spoon, 1 to 2 minutes.

Remove from the heat, let cool, then use right away or transfer to an airtight container and refrigerate for up to 4 days.

Cook's Notes

For a deeper umami flavor, whisk ½ tsp dashi powder with the other ingredients or finish with 1 tsp toasted sesame seeds.

Mirin is a sweet, rice-based Japanese cooking wine that naturally caramelizes as it cooks, so keep the heat gentle to avoid burning.

Nutrition Values (per 1-Tbsp serving): Energy (kJ) ~63 kJ, Calories ~15 kcal, Fat 0 g, Saturated Fat 0 g, Carbohydrate ~3 g, Sugar ~2 g, Dietary Fiber 0 g, Protein ~0.3 g, Cholesterol 0 mg, Sodium ~320 mg

Nước Chấm (Vietnamese Dipping Sauce)

MAKES ¾ CUP (175 ML)

¼ cup (60 ml) water
1½ Tbsp rice vinegar
1½ Tbsp sugar
3 Tbsp Asian fish sauce
2 Tbsp fresh lime juice
½ fresh red Thai chile, finely chopped, or ½ tsp Thai chile paste
1 garlic clove, minced
2 Tbsp finely shredded carrot

To make the sauce, in a small saucepan over medium heat, combine the water, vinegar, and sugar. Bring to a gentle boil, stirring until the sugar dissolves. Remove from the heat and let cool completely.

Stir in the fish sauce, lime juice, chile, garlic, and carrot. Transfer to an airtight container and refrigerate for at least 30 minutes before using or up to 3 days.

Nutrition Values (per 1-Tbsp serving): Energy (kJ) ~33 kJ, Calories ~8 kcal, Fat 0 g, Saturated Fat 0 g, Carbohydrate ~2 g, Sugar ~1.5 g, Dietary Fiber 0 g, Protein ~0.2 g, Cholesterol 0 mg, Sodium ~320 mg (mostly from fish sauce)

Creamy Mustard Sauce

MAKES ABOUT 1 CUP (240 ML)

1 Tbsp unsalted butter

1 small shallot, finely minced

½ cup (120 ml) dry white wine or chicken broth

¾ cup (175 ml) heavy cream

2 Tbsp Dijon mustard

1 tsp whole-grain mustard

1 tsp Worcestershire sauce (optional)

Kosher salt and freshly ground pepper

1 tsp fresh lemon juice

1 Tbsp chopped fresh herbs, such as tarragon, flat-leaf parsley, or chives

To make the sauce, in a small saucepan over medium heat, melt the butter. Add the shallot and cook, stirring, until softened and fragrant, about 2 minutes. Pour in the wine and simmer until reduced by half.

Turn down the heat to low, stir in the cream and both mustards, and whisk until smooth. Simmer gently, stirring occasionally, until the sauce thickens slightly, 3 to 5 minutes.

Stir in the Worcestershire sauce (if using) and season with salt, pepper, and the lemon juice. Remove from the heat, stir in the herbs, and serve at once.

Nutrition Values (per 2-Tbsp serving): Energy (kJ) ~377 kJ, Calories ~90 kcal, Fat ~8 g, Saturated Fat ~5 g, Carbohydrate ~2 g, Sugar ~1 g, Dietary Fiber 0 g, Protein ~0.5 g, Cholesterol ~25 mg, Sodium ~180 mg

Italian Salsa Verde

MAKES ABOUT 1 CUP (240 G)

1 cup (12 g) lightly packed fresh flat-leaf parsley leaves, finely chopped

2 Tbsp capers, rinsed and chopped

3 or 4 olive oil–packed anchovy fillets, chopped

2 garlic cloves, minced

1 Tbsp red wine vinegar or fresh lemon juice

½ cup (120 ml) extra virgin olive oil

Kosher salt and freshly ground pepper

To mince the ingredients, on a cutting board, combine the parsley, capers, anchovies, and garlic. Using a large knife, finely chop the ingredients together until a rough paste forms. (Alternatively, briefly pulse the ingredients together in a mini food processor.)

To finish the sauce, transfer the mixture to a small bowl and stir in the vinegar. While whisking constantly, slowly drizzle in the oil, continuing to whisk until the salsa has a spoonable consistency.

Taste and adjust the seasoning with salt, pepper, and vinegar if needed. Let stand for 15 minutes before serving to allow the flavors to meld.

For a looser texture, whisk in a splash of warm water before serving. Store leftover salsa in an airtight container in the refrigerator for up to 3 days; bring to room temperature before using.

Nutrition Values (per 2-Tbsp serving): Energy (kJ) ~502 kJ, Calories ~120 kcal, Fat ~12 g, Saturated Fat ~2 g, Carbohydrate ~1 g, Sugar ~0 g, Dietary Fiber ~0.5 g, Protein ~1 g, Cholesterol ~5 mg (from anchovies), Sodium ~250 mg (mostly from capers and anchovies)

Mushroom Herb Sauce

MAKES ABOUT 2 CUPS (480G)

2 Tbsp unsalted butter or olive oil

2 shallots, finely chopped

2 garlic cloves, minced

1 lb (450 g) mixed mushrooms, such as cremini, shiitake, and button, stem ends trimmed and sliced

Kosher salt and freshly ground pepper

½ cup (120 ml) dry white wine or chicken broth

½ cup (120 ml) heavy cream

1 tsp Dijon mustard

1 Tbsp chopped fresh parsley, plus more for garnish

1 Tbsp chopped fresh tarragon leaves, or
1 tsp chopped fresh thyme leaves

To cook the aromatics, in a large skillet over medium heat, melt the butter. Add the shallots and cook, stirring, until softened, about 2 minutes. Stir in the garlic and cook, stirring, until fragrant, about 1 minute.

Add the mushrooms to the skillet and season with salt and pepper. Cook, stirring, until they release their liquid and turn golden brown, 8 to 10 minutes.

Pour the wine into the skillet and bring to a simmer, stirring to scrape up any browned bits from the pan bottom. Continue to simmer, stirring, until the liquid has reduced by about three-fourths, 3 to 4 minutes.

To finish the sauce, turn down the heat to low and add the cream and mustard. Simmer gently, stirring occasionally, until slightly thickened, 2 to 3 minutes. Stir in both herbs, taste, and adjust the seasoning with salt and pepper if needed. Remove from the heat and serve at once, garnished with parsley.

Nutrition Values (per ¼ cup/60 g serving): Energy (kJ) ~335 kJ, Calories ~80 kcal, Fat ~6 g, Saturated Fat ~3 g, Carbohydrate ~4 g, Sugar ~1 g, Dietary Fiber ~1 g, Protein ~2 g, Cholesterol ~15 mg, Sodium ~100 mg (varies with added salt and mustard)

Garlic Herb Butter

MAKES ABOUT ½ CUP (120 G)

½ cup unsalted butter, at cool room temperature

2 garlic cloves, minced

1 Tbsp minced mixed fresh herbs, such as flat-leaf parsley, thyme, oregano, basil, tarragon, and/or chives

¼ tsp kosher salt

½ tsp freshly ground pepper

To make the butter, in a bowl, combine the butter, garlic, herbs, salt, and pepper. Using a fork, mash the ingredients together until well mixed.

Scrape the butter onto the center of a square of plastic wrap and, using the fork, shape the butter into a rough wide strip. Bring the plastic wrap up over the butter and use it to shape the butter into an even log about 1½ inches (4 cm) in diameter and 4 inches (10 cm) long. Roll up the butter tightly in the plastic wrap and twist the ends to seal.

Refrigerate the butter until chilled and firm, about 2 hours, before using. It will keep for up to 2 weeks.

Nutrition Values (per 1-Tbsp serving): Energy (kJ) ~418 kJ, Calories ~100 kcal, Fat ~11 g, Saturated Fat ~7 g, Carbohydrate ~0.5 g, Sugar ~0 g, Dietary Fiber 0 g, Protein ~0.3 g, Cholesterol ~30 mg, Sodium ~60 mg (from salt and herbs)

Sun-Dried Tomato Butter

MAKES ABOUT ¾ CUP (155 G)

½ cup (110 g) unsalted butter, at cool room temperature

⅓ cup (40 g) drained sun-dried tomatoes in oil, minced

2 garlic cloves, minced

1 tsp minced fresh thyme leaves

1 tsp fresh lemon juice

Kosher salt and freshly ground pepper

To make the butter, in a small bowl, combine the butter, tomatoes, garlic, thyme, and lemon juice. Season with salt and pepper. Using a fork, mash the ingredients together until well mixed.

Scrape the butter onto the center of a square of plastic wrap and, using the fork, shape the butter into a rough wide strip. Bring the plastic wrap up over the butter and use it to shape the butter into an even log about 1½ inches (4 cm) in diameter and 4 inches (10 cm) long. Roll up the butter tightly in the plastic wrap and twist the ends to seal.

Refrigerate the butter until chilled and firm, about 2 hours, before using. It will keep for up to 2 weeks.

Nutrition Values (per 1-Tbsp serving): Energy (kJ) ~377 kJ, Calories ~90 kcal, Fat ~9 g, Saturated Fat ~5 g, Carbohydrate ~1 g, Sugar ~0.5 g, Dietary Fiber 0 g, Protein ~0.3 g, Cholesterol ~20 mg, Sodium ~70 mg (varies with added salt and sundried tomatoes)

Lemon Miso Butter

MAKES ABOUT ½ CUP (110 G)

½ cup (110 g) unsalted butter, at cool room temperature

1½ tsp finely grated lemon zest

1 tsp white miso

1 tsp fresh lemon juice

Kosher salt and freshly ground pepper

To make the butter, in a bowl, combine the butter, lemon zest, miso, and lemon juice. Season with salt and pepper. Using a fork, mash the ingredients together until well mixed.

Scrape the butter onto the center of a square of plastic wrap and, using the fork, shape the butter into a rough wide strip. Bring the plastic wrap up over the butter and use it to shape the butter into an even log about 1½ inches (4 cm) in diameter. Roll up the butter tightly in the plastic wrap and twist the ends to seal.

Refrigerate the butter until chilled and firm, about 2 hours, before using. It will keep for up to 2 weeks.

Nutrition Values (per 1-Tbsp serving): Energy (kJ) ~418 kJ, Calories ~100 kcal, Fat ~11 g, Saturated Fat ~7 g, Carbohydrate ~0.5 g, Sugar ~0 g, Dietary Fiber 0 g, Protein ~0.3 g, Cholesterol ~30 mg, Sodium ~90 mg (mostly from miso and added salt)

Side Dishes

Creamy Mashed Potatoes

MAKES 4 SERVINGS

1½ lb (680 g) starchy potatoes, such as Yukon Gold or russets, peeled and cut into 1-inch (2.5-cm) chunks

Kosher salt and freshly ground pepper

2 Tbsp unsalted butter, at room temperature

½ cup (120 ml) whole milk, warmed

To cook the potatoes, fill a large pot three-fourths full with water and add the potatoes and 1 Tbsp salt. Bring to a boil over medium-high heat, then turn down the heat to medium-low and boil gently, stirring occasionally, until tender, 12 to 15 minutes.

To mash the potatoes, drain the potatoes into a colander. Return the potatoes to the pot and, using a potato masher, mash until nearly smooth. Add the butter, milk, and 1 tsp salt and continue to mash until fully incorporated. Then switch to a fork and beat the potatoes until whipped and smooth.

Taste and adjust the seasoning with salt if needed and with pepper. Transfer to a warmed serving dish and serve at once.

Cook's Notes

For a richer flavor, replace the milk with heavy cream or sour cream. Or, fold finely chopped fresh chives or crumbled crisply cooked bacon into the mashed potatoes.

For garlic mashed potatoes, peel the cloves from a whole head of roasted garlic, add them to the drained potatoes, and mash the garlic along with the potatoes.

Nutrition Values (per serving): Energy (kJ) ~879 kJ, Calories ~210 kcal, Fat ~6 g, Saturated Fat ~3.5 g, Carbohydrate ~34 g, Sugar ~3 g, Dietary Fiber ~3 g, Protein ~4 g, Cholesterol ~15 mg, Sodium ~450 mg (includes added salt during cooking)

Winter Squash Puree

MAKES 4 SERVINGS

1½ lb (680 g) butternut, Red Kuri, or kabocha squash, peeled, seeded, and cut into 1-inch (2.5-cm) cubes

1 Tbsp olive oil

Kosher salt and freshly ground pepper

½ cup (120 ml) heavy cream or whole milk, warmed

To roast the squash, preheat the oven to 400°F (200°C). On a large sheet pan, toss the squash cubes with the oil, coating evenly, and season generously with salt and pepper. Spread the cubes in a single layer.

Roast the squash, stirring once or twice during cooking, until tender and lightly caramelized, 25 to 30 minutes.

To puree the squash, transfer the hot roasted squash to a food processor or blender. Add the cream and process, stopping the machine and scraping down the sides of the bowl as needed, until completely smooth and creamy. Taste and adjust the seasoning with salt and pepper if needed.

Transfer to a warmed serving dish and serve at once.

Cook's Notes

For a refined finish, add a sprinkle of freshly grated nutmeg, a drizzle of brown butter, several toasted pumpkin seeds, or a fresh thyme sprig.

Nutrition Values (per serving): Energy (kJ) ~711 kJ, Calories ~170 kcal, Fat ~9 g, Saturated Fat ~5 g, Carbohydrate ~22 g, Sugar ~8 g, Dietary Fiber ~4 g, Protein ~2 g, Cholesterol ~30 mg, Sodium ~250 mg (depends on added salt)

Smashed Parsnips

MAKES 4 SERVINGS

4 large parsnips, peeled and cut into 1-inch (2.5-cm) chunks

Kosher salt and freshly ground pepper

½ cup (120 ml) heavy cream, warmed

¼ tsp freshly grated nutmeg

To cook the parsnips, fill a large pot three-fourths full with water and add the parsnips and 1 Tbsp salt. Bring to a boil over medium-high heat, then turn down the heat to medium-low and boil gently, stirring occasionally, until tender but not mushy, 12 to 15 minutes.

To smash the parsnips, drain the parsnips into a colander. Return the parsnips to the pot and, using a potato masher, mash until nearly smooth while slowly adding the cream and nutmeg. Taste and adjust the seasoning with salt if needed and with pepper.

Transfer to a warmed serving dish and serve at once.

Nutrition Values (per serving): Energy (kJ) ~795 kJ, Calories ~190 kcal, Fat ~9 g, Saturated Fat ~5 g, Carbohydrate ~26 g, Sugar ~7 g, Dietary Fiber ~5 g, Protein ~2 g, Cholesterol ~30 mg, Sodium ~300 mg (depends on added salt)

Grilled Vegetables

MAKES 4 SERVINGS

1 bunch asparagus, woody ends trimmed

1 medium zucchini or summer squash, cut lengthwise into strips ¼ inch (6 mm) thick

1 small eggplant, sliced into rounds ¼ inch (6 mm) thick

1 red bell pepper, seeded, and cut into wide strips

1 small red onion, cut into 8 wedges

Extra virgin olive oil, for drizzling

Kosher salt and freshly ground black pepper

Balsamic vinegar or fresh lemon juice, for drizzling (optional)

Chopped fresh basil or parsley, for garnish (optional)

To prep the vegetables, on a large sheet pan, toss the asparagus, zucchini, eggplant, bell pepper, and onion with a drizzle of oil, coating evenly, then season generously with salt and pepper.

Prepare a charcoal or gas grill for direct cooking over medium-high heat (400° to 450°F/200° to 230°C). When the grill is ready, brush the grill grates clean.

To grill the vegetables, place them in a single layer on the grill grates directly over the fire, close the lid, and grill, turning occasionally, until nicely etched with grill marks and tender-crisp, about 4 minutes for the asparagus, zucchini, and eggplant and 10 minutes for the bell pepper and red onion.

As the vegetables finish cooking, transfer them to a platter. When all the vegetables are cooked, drizzle them with vinegar and garnish with herbs, if using. Serve warm or at room temperature.

Nutrition Values (per serving): Energy (kJ) ~502 kJ, Calories ~120 kcal, Fat ~8 g, Saturated Fat ~1 g, Carbohydrate ~12 g, Sugar ~6 g, Dietary Fiber ~4 g, Protein ~3 g, Cholesterol 0 mg, Sodium ~150 mg (depends on added salt)

Roasted Potatoes, Root Vegetables & Winter Squash

MAKES 4 SERVINGS

1½ to 2 lb (680 to 900 g) potatoes, sweet potatoes, carrots, parsnips, and/or winter squashes, peeled, seeded (squashes), and cut into 1-inch (2.5-cm) chunks

2 Tbsp olive oil

1 tsp kosher salt

½ tsp freshly ground pepper

Preheat the oven to 425°F (220°C).

To prep the vegetables, on a large sheet pan, toss the vegetables with the oil, coating evenly, then season with the salt and pepper. Spread the vegetables in a single layer.

Roast the vegetables, turning once or twice during cooking, until tender and caramelized or golden brown at the edges, 30 to 40 minutes.

Transfer to a serving dish and taste and adjust the seasoning with salt if needed. Serve warm.

Cook's Notes

For extra flavor, toss the vegetables with chopped fresh herbs, such as thyme or rosemary before roasting. Or finish with a sprinkle of flaky sea salt and a squeeze of fresh lemon juice.

Nutrition Values (per serving): Energy (kJ) ~753 kJ, Calories ~180 kcal, Fat ~5 g, Saturated Fat ~1 g, Carbohydrate ~32 g, Sugar ~6 g, Dietary Fiber ~5 g, Protein ~3 g, Cholesterol 0 mg, Sodium ~300 mg (depends on added salt)

Stir-Fried Greens

MAKES 4 SERVINGS

1 to 2 Tbsp olive oil

2 garlic cloves, minced

1½ lb (680 g) greens, such as kale, chard, collards, or spinach, tough stems removed and leaves roughly chopped

Kosher salt and freshly ground pepper

To cook the greens, in a large skillet or wok over medium-high heat, warm the oil. Add the garlic and cook, stirring occasionally, until fragrant but not browned, about 30 seconds.

Add the greens and cook, stirring and tossing constantly, until wilted but still vibrant. Sturdier greens, such as kale, collards, and chard, will take 5 to 7 minutes, while tender greens, such as spinach, will take 2 to 3 minutes. Season with salt and pepper and toss gently.

Transfer to a serving dish and serve at once.

Cook's Notes

Cook tender baby bok choy or broccolini (trimmed of tough stems) using this method. Cook them both until tender but still vibrant green. The bok choy will take about 3 minutes, and the broccolini will take about 5 minutes.

Season the cooked greens with 1 tsp peeled and minced fresh ginger or garnish with toasted sesame seeds, chopped fresh herbs, or a squeeze of fresh lemon juice.

Nutrition Values (per serving): Energy (kJ) ~377 kJ, Calories ~90 kcal, Fat ~5 g, Saturated Fat ~0.8 g, Carbohydrate ~8 g, Sugar ~1 g, Dietary Fiber ~4 g, Protein ~4 g, Cholesterol 0 mg, Sodium ~150 mg (varies with added salt)

Garlicky Green Rice

MAKES 4 SERVINGS

GREEN SAUCE

½ cup (115 g) chopped fresh cilantro

¼ cup (60 ml) water

2 garlic cloves, chopped

Juice of ½ lime

1½ Tbsp chicken broth concentrate or chicken bouillon

1 tsp kosher salt

½ tsp freshly ground pepper

1½ cups (300 g) medium-grain white rice, rinsed under cold running water and drained

2 cups (475 ml) water

To make the green sauce, in a blender, combine the cilantro, water, garlic, lime juice, chicken broth concentrate, salt, and pepper and blend until smooth. Taste and adjust the seasoning with lime juice if needed.

To cook the rice, in a small saucepan, combine the rice, water, and the green sauce and stir to mix. Cover, place over medium-high heat, and bring to a boil. Turn down the heat to low and cook, covered, until the liquid is absorbed and the rice is tender, about 20 minutes.

Remove from the heat and set aside, covered, for 10 minutes. Uncover, fluff the rice with a fork, and serve warm.

Nutrition Values (per serving): Energy (kJ) ~1172 kJ, Calories ~280 kcal, Fat ~3 g, Saturated Fat ~0.5 g, Carbohydrate ~55 g, Sugar ~1 g, Dietary Fiber ~1 g, Protein ~5 g, Cholesterol 0 mg, Sodium ~500 mg (mostly from chicken broth concentrate and added salt)

Garlic Bread

MAKES 4 SERVINGS

½ cup (110 g) unsalted butter, at room temperature

3 large garlic cloves, minced

2 tsp Italian seasoning

1 tsp garlic powder

½ tsp sweet paprika

½ tsp kosher salt

¼ tsp freshly ground pepper

1 large loaf Italian or French bread, split horizontally

¼ cup (8 g) grated Parmesan cheese

Preheat the oven to 400°F (200°C). Line a large sheet pan with parchment paper or aluminum foil.

To make the garlic butter spread, in a small bowl, combine the butter, minced garlic, Italian seasoning, garlic powder, paprika, salt, and pepper. Using a fork, mash the ingredients together until well mixed.

Place the bread halves cut-side up on the prepared sheet pan. Spread the butter mixture evenly over the cut sides, dividing it evenly, then sprinkle evenly with the Parmesan.

Bake the bread until hot and crisp and the edges are browned, about 10 minutes.

Transfer to a cutting board and cut crosswise into pieces. Serve at once.

Cook's Notes

To make extra-cheesy garlic bread, top the Parmesan layer with 1 cup (120 g) shredded low-moisture mozzarella cheese before baking.

Nutrition Values (per serving): Energy (kJ) ~1297 kJ, Calories ~310 kcal, Fat ~18 g, Saturated Fat ~10 g, Carbohydrate ~30 g, Sugar ~1 g, Dietary Fiber ~1.5 g, Protein ~6 g, Cholesterol ~45 mg, Sodium ~520 mg

2 Weeknight Winners

“Weeknight cooking is where real life happens.”

–Kristin

If there's one truth I've learned from decades in the kitchen, both the professional kind filled with stainless steel and the home kind filled with backpacks, grocery bags, and the occasional unmatched lunch-box lid, it's that weeknight cooking is where real life happens. It's where hunger meets reality, where intention meets time, and where we, as home cooks, try our best to feed the people we love without losing our minds somewhere between the cutting board and the sink.

As a chef, I've spent years developing recipes meant to inspire, delight, and sometimes even challenge. But as a mom, I've learned that at 6:30 p.m. on a Tuesday, inspiration looks a little different. It looks like meals that come together quickly but still feel nourishing. It looks like flavors big enough to wake up tired taste buds but familiar enough that no one pushes away their plate. It looks like vegetables that actually get eaten, sauces that practically make themselves, and proteins that cook up without fuss. And it looks like the tiny victories that only another home cook would understand, like using up some produce before it wilts, getting a balanced meal on the table in under thirty minutes, or receiving a wholehearted "this is really good" from someone who said they weren't that hungry.

This chapter is filled with those kinds of recipes—the ones that save you on the busiest nights, surprise you with how simple they really are, and remind you that delicious doesn't have to mean complicated. These are dishes built on smart technique, good ingredients, and the belief that food should make your life easier, not harder.

More than anything, I hope these Weeknight Winners bring a little calm to the chaos. I hope they give you moments, however small, of pride, comfort, joy, or connection around your dinner table. Because feeding our families, our friends, and even ourselves isn't just about getting dinner done. It's also about caring in the most everyday, extraordinary way. Here's to winning the weeknight, one delicious recipe at a time.

—Kristin

Chicken Riggies

This comforting pasta dish has become the ultimate family favorite in the home of Kristin Bryan, head of Culinary Innovation. It fits as easily into a busy Tuesday night as it does a more leisurely Sunday dinner. A creamy sauce—rich but approachable and infused with just the right amount of heat from cherry peppers—clings to the rigatoni. For extra spice, add more cherry peppers or a pinch of red pepper flakes. For a milder version, swap in sweet cherry peppers.

MAKES 4 TO 6 SERVINGS

1 lb (450 g) rigatoni

1½ lb (680 g) boneless, skinless chicken breasts, cut into bite-size pieces

Kosher salt and freshly ground black pepper

2 Tbsp olive oil

1 Tbsp unsalted butter

1 medium yellow onion, finely chopped

3 garlic cloves, minced

1 (8-oz/225-g) jar hot cherry peppers, drained with brine reserved, then seeded and sliced

2 cups (500 g) marinara sauce

1 tablespoon sugar (optional)

½ to ¾ cup (120 to 175 ml) heavy cream

½ cup (15 g) grated Parmesan cheese, plus more for serving

2 Tbsp chopped fresh flat-leaf parsley

To cook the pasta, bring a large pot of salted water to a boil over high heat. Add the rigatoni and boil gently, stirring occasionally, until al dente, about 9 minutes or according to package directions. Scoop out ½ cup (120 ml) of the pasta water, then drain the pasta into a colander and set the reserved water and pasta aside separately.

While the pasta cooks, cook the chicken. Season the chicken pieces all over with salt and black pepper. In a large skillet over medium-high heat, warm the oil. When the oil is shimmering, add the chicken and sear, turning once or twice, until golden and just cooked through, 5 to 7 minutes. Transfer to a plate.

To make the sauce, turn down the heat to medium and add the butter and onion to the skillet. Cook, stirring often, until the onion is softened, about 5 minutes. Stir in the garlic and cherry peppers and cook, stirring often, until fragrant, about 1 minute. Stir in the marinara sauce and a splash of cherry pepper brine and simmer, stirring occasionally, until the sauce thickens slightly, 5 to 7 minutes. Stir in the sugar, if using.

Turn down the heat to low and stir in the cream, starting with ½ cup (120 ml) and adding more for a creamier sauce. Return the chicken and any juices on the plate to the skillet and simmer gently, stirring occasionally, until the chicken is heated through, 3 to 4 minutes.

To assemble and serve, add the cooked rigatoni and the Parmesan to the skillet and stir and toss to coat evenly. Add the reserved pasta water, a splash at a time, stirring after each addition, until the sauce clings to the pasta and the pasta is heated through. Taste and adjust the seasoning with salt and ground pepper. Transfer to a platter, sprinkle with the parsley and some Parmesan, and serve at once.

Nutrition Values (per serving for 6 servings): Energy (kJ) ~2259 kJ, Calories ~540 kcal, Fat ~22 g, Saturated Fat ~10 g, Carbohydrate ~50 g, Sugar ~6 g, Dietary Fiber ~3 g, Protein ~38 g, Cholesterol ~115 mg, Sodium ~950 mg

Pesto Heirloom Tomato Grilled Cheese

Thick slices of artisanal bread are layered with a trio of melty cheeses, fragrant pesto, and juicy heirloom tomatoes, creating a sandwich that's both rustic and indulgent. Perfect for a cozy lunch, an easy dinner, or a casual weekend bite, this grilled cheese is simple to assemble yet feels special, turning an ordinary meal into something memorable and satisfying.

MAKES 4 SANDWICHES

8 large slices artisanal bread, such as levain or sourdough, each about ½ inch (12 mm) thick

About ¾ cup (180 g) basil pesto, homemade (page 43) or store-bought

1 cup (120 g) shredded sharp white Cheddar cheese

1½ cups (180 g) shredded Havarti cheese

2 oz (55 g) Parmesan cheese, grated

8 to 12 thick slices ripe heirloom tomato (depending on size of tomatoes)

Kosher salt and freshly ground pepper

To assemble the sandwiches, spread one side of each bread slice thickly with the pesto. Lay four of the bread slices, pesto-side down, in a large skillet. In a bowl, toss together the three cheeses. Add about half of the cheese mixture to the four bread slices in the skillet, dividing it evenly and spreading it in an even layer. Top each bread slice with the tomato slices, dividing them evenly. Top the tomatoes evenly with the remaining cheese. Cap each sandwich with a bread slice, pesto-side up.

To cook the sandwiches, place the pan over medium-low heat and cook until the bottom of each sandwich is browned and the cheese starts to melt, about 3 minutes. Carefully turn each sandwich and continue to cook until the second side is browned and the cheese is melted and gooey, about 3 minutes longer.

To serve, transfer the sandwiches to plates, cut in half if you like, and serve at once.

Nutrition Values (per sandwich): Energy (kJ) ~2176 kJ, Calories ~520 kcal, Fat ~32 g, Saturated Fat ~16 g, Carbohydrate ~38 g, Sugar ~3 g, Dietary Fiber ~2 g, Protein ~20 g, Cholesterol ~65 mg, Sodium ~780 mg

Cucumber Gazpacho with Grilled Shrimp

Refreshing and effortlessly elegant, this cucumber gazpacho pairs beautifully with grilled shrimp or, for a fancier presentation, a mound of lump crabmeat. Creamy Greek yogurt balances the crisp cucumber and fresh summer herbs, and a touch of white wine vinegar adds brightness. Perfect for a light warm-weather dinner or a weekend lunch, it's a dish that feels special without any fuss. If you like, dress it up with simple toppings, like chopped tomato and crunchy croutons.

MAKES 4 SERVINGS

1 lb (450 g) Persian (about 6) or English cucumbers, chopped

1 cup plus 1 Tbsp (240 g) plain Greek yogurt

2 Tbsp extra virgin olive oil, plus more for drizzling

¼ cup (10 g) chopped mixed fresh summer herbs, such as mint, chives, and flat-leaf parsley

1 Tbsp white wine vinegar

Pinch of kosher salt

Grilled Shrimp Kebabs (page 39)

To make the gazpacho, in a blender, combine the cucumbers, yogurt, oil, herbs, vinegar, and salt and blend on high speed until very smooth. Transfer to an airtight container and refrigerate until well chilled, about 1 hour.

While the gazpacho is chilling, grill the shrimp kebabs.

To serve, taste the gazpacho and adjust the seasoning with salt if needed (chilling mutes flavors, so you may need to add more). Divide the gazpacho evenly among four bowls. Slide the shrimp from the skewers, and top each bowl with an equal number of shrimp. Drizzle with olive oil and serve.

Nutrition Values (per serving): Energy (kJ) ~879 kJ, Calories ~210 kcal, Fat ~10 g, Saturated Fat ~2 g, Carbohydrate ~9 g, Sugar ~5 g, Dietary Fiber ~2 g, Protein ~20 g, Cholesterol ~115 mg, Sodium ~420 mg

Chickpea, Spinach & Sweet Potato Curry

This plant-based curry is both hearty and nourishing. Sweet potatoes and chickpeas soak up a fragrant blend of cumin, coriander, turmeric, and ginger, while red pepper flakes add gentle warmth. Coconut milk and lemon juice balance the spices, and fresh spinach and cilantro add freshness. Served over steamed rice, it's a quick and satisfying dinner that's full of flavor and color.

MAKES 4 SERVINGS

1 Tbsp vegetable oil or ghee

½ yellow onion, finely chopped

2 garlic cloves, minced

2 tsp peeled and finely grated fresh ginger

1 tsp ground cumin

1 tsp ground coriander

1 tsp ground turmeric

½ tsp red pepper flakes, plus more if needed

Kosher salt and freshly ground black pepper

1 (13.5–fl oz/405-ml) can coconut milk, well shaken

¾ cup (175 ml) water

1 large orange sweet potato (about 12 oz/340 g), peeled and cut into ½-inch (12-mm) cubes

1 (15-oz/425-g) can chickpeas, drained and rinsed

Juice of 1 lemon

5 oz (140 g) roughly chopped baby spinach (about 4 cups)

¼ cup (10 g) chopped fresh cilantro, plus more for garnish

Steamed rice, for serving

To make the curry, in a medium saucepan over medium heat, warm the oil. Add the onion and cook, stirring, until softened and starting to brown, about 5 minutes. Stir in the garlic and ginger, then add the cumin, coriander, turmeric, and red pepper flakes. Season generously with salt and black pepper and stir to mix well.

Add the coconut milk, water, sweet potato, chickpeas, and lemon juice to the saucepan. Increase the heat to medium-high and bring to a boil. Turn down the heat to medium-low, cover partially, and simmer, stirring occasionally, until the sweet potato is tender, about 20 minutes. If the curry seems too dry, add a bit more water.

Taste and adjust the seasoning with salt, black pepper, and red pepper flakes if needed. Stir in the spinach and cilantro and cook just until the spinach wilts, about 1 minute.

To serve, divide the rice among four shallow bowls. Ladle the hot curry over the rice, garnish with more cilantro, and serve at once.

Nutrition Values (per serving): Energy (kJ) ~1339 kJ, Calories ~320 kcal, Fat ~16 g, Saturated Fat ~10 g, Carbohydrate ~34 g, Sugar ~8 g, Dietary Fiber ~8 g, Protein ~8 g, Cholesterol 0 mg (plant-based), Sodium ~420 mg

Pesto Panko Chicken with Roasted Potatoes & Green Beans

Pesto isn't just for pasta. Here it's the star of crispy, golden chicken. Spread over chicken breasts, it helps the panko and mozzarella stick, creating a flavorful, crunchy crust while keeping the meat juicy and aromatic. The chicken is roasted alongside tender Yukon Gold potatoes and bright green beans for an all-in-one, weeknight-friendly meal.

MAKES 4 SERVINGS

1½ lb (680 g) Yukon Gold potatoes, unpeeled, cut into ½-inch (12-mm) chunks

Olive oil, for drizzling

Kosher salt and freshly ground pepper

1 cup (60 g) panko breadcrumbs

1 cup (120 g) shredded low-moisture mozzarella cheese

4 boneless, skinless chicken breasts (about 1½ lb (680 g), pounded to an even thickness (see page 38)

About ½ cup (120 g) basil pesto, homemade (page 43) or store-bought

12 oz (340 g) green beans, trimmed

1 Tbsp unsalted butter

⅓ cup (35 g) sliced almonds, lightly toasted

1 lemon, cut into wedges

Position one oven rack in the middle and one in the upper third of the oven and preheat the oven to 450°F (230°C).

To prep the potatoes, on a large sheet pan, toss the potatoes with a drizzle of oil, coating evenly, then season generously with salt and pepper. Spread in a single layer.

To prep the chicken, in a bowl, combine the panko, mozzarella, a drizzle of oil, and a pinch each of salt and pepper and stir to mix.Lightly oil a sheet pan and place the chicken breasts on the pan. Brush the top of each breast with a thin layer of pesto then mound the panko mixture on the top of each breast, dividing it evenly and pressing it to adhere.

To roast the potatoes and chicken, slide the sheet pan with the potatoes onto the top rack of the oven and the sheet pan with the chicken onto the middle rack. Roast the potatoes, stirring halfway through cooking, until browned and tender, 20 to 25 minutes. Roast the chicken until golden brown and opaque throughout, 20 to 22 minutes.

To make the green beans, while the potatoes and chicken cook, fill a small saucepan three-fourths full with salted water and bring to a boil over high heat. Add the green beans, turn down the heat to medium, and boil gently until tender-crisp, 2 to 5 minutes. Drain well and transfer to a bowl. Add the butter, almonds, and a squeeze of lemon juice and toss to coat evenly. Season with salt and pepper.

To serve, divide the potatoes, chicken, and green beans among four plates. Serve at once, with the remaining lemon wedges on the side.

Nutrition Values (per serving): Energy (kJ) 3556 kJ, Calories 850 kcal, Fat 52 g, Saturated Fat 13 g, Carbohydrate 54 g, Sugar 8 g, Dietary Fiber 11 g, Protein 49 g, Cholesterol 150 mg, Sodium 640 mg

Samosa Smash Tacos with Chutney

Here, spiced potatoes and peas are smashed onto warm flour tortillas, bringing the flavors of a traditional samosa filling to easy-to-make smash tacos. Shredded paneer, zesty red onion, fresh cilantro, and a squeeze of lime add brightness, while a drizzle each of chutney and yogurt provides tang and creaminess.

MAKES 8 TACOS; 4 SERVINGS

1 lb (450 g) Yukon Gold potatoes, peeled and cut into 1-inch (2.5-cm) chunks

Kosher salt

Vegetable oil, for drizzling and brushing

1 jalapeño chile, seeded and minced

½ cup (65 g) frozen petite peas

1 tsp ground cumin

½ tsp ground coriander

½ tsp chili powder

Juice of ½ lime

2 Tbsp chopped fresh cilantro, plus more for garnish

3 oz (85 g) paneer cheese, shredded on the large holes of a box grater-shredder

8 (6-inch/15-cm) flour tortillas

½ cup (60 g) thinly sliced red onion

Mint, cilantro, or tamarind chutney, for serving

Plain yogurt (not Greek), for serving

To cook the potatoes, fill a saucepan with water and add the potatoes and a big pinch of salt. Bring to a boil over high heat, then turn down the heat to medium and boil gently, stirring occasionally, until the potatoes are tender, 8 to 10 minutes. Drain well and set aside.

To make the samosa filling, return the saucepan to medium heat and add a drizzle of oil. Add the jalapeño and peas and cook, stirring, for 2 minutes. Remove the pan from the heat and add the potatoes, cumin, coriander, and chili powder. Using a fork, smash the mixture together, adding a little water to loosen the mixture. It should be a thick paste. Transfer to a bowl and stir in the lime juice, cilantro, and paneer.

To prep the tacos, place a large skillet over medium heat. When the skillet is hot, lightly brush the bottom with oil. Working in batches, add the tortillas in a single layer to the hot pan and toast the underside until golden brown, about 1 minute. Transfer the tortillas toasted-side up to a clean work surface. Divide the potato mixture between the tortillas, spreading it in a thin, even layer. Divide the onion slices evenly among the tortillas, pressing them into the potato mixture.

To cook the tacos, return the skillet to medium heat and lightly brush with oil. Working in batches to avoid crowding, place the tortillas, potato mixture side down, into the skillet and press the tortillas into the pan with a spatula. Cook until the potato mixture is browned, about 2 minutes. Brush the top of each tortilla lightly with oil, then flip and cook until crisp on the second side, about 1 minute longer. Transfer to a platter, potato-side up, then repeat with the rest of the tortillas, adding more oil as needed.

To serve, garnish each taco with cilantro and a drizzle each of chutney and yogurt. Serve warm.

Nutrition Values (per 2-taco serving): Energy (kJ) ~1757 kJ, Calories ~420 kcal, Fat ~14 g, Saturated Fat ~5 g, Carbohydrate ~60 g, Sugar ~6 g, Dietary Fiber ~6 g, Protein ~11 g, Cholesterol ~15 mg, Sodium ~680 mg

Currywurst Tteokbokki with Rice Cakes

Daniel Kim of the HelloFresh Culinary Team draws inspiration from the tasty street foods of his childhood in Korea and his time in Berlin, Germany. Memories of tteokbokki—spicy sweet rice cakes—paired with Berlin's currywurst sparked his fascination with bold, saucy flavors. This recipe celebrates those formative culinary experiences, combining spice and irresistible umami to honor the streets that shaped his palate and the flavors he continues to crave across continents.

MAKES 2 SERVINGS

7 oz (200 g) Korean cylinder-shaped rice cakes (tteok)

2 soft-boiled eggs (optional)

1 Tbsp vegetable oil

2 bratwursts (about ½ lb/225g)

2 Tbsp ketchup

1 Tbsp gochujang (Korean fermented chile paste)

1½ tsp sugar

1 tsp soy sauce

½ tsp gochugaru (Korean chile flakes)

½ tsp curry powder, plus more for garnish

1 garlic clove, minced

1 cup (240 ml) water

1 tsp sesame seeds, toasted

1 scallion, thinly sliced on the diagonal, white and green parts separated

If the rice cakes are firm, put them into a medium bowl, add warm water to cover, and set aside to soak for 10 to 15 minutes.

To soft-boil the eggs, fill a saucepan with enough water to cover the eggs completely and bring to a boil over high heat. Fill a bowl with ice and water for an ice bath and set it near the stove. Using a slotted spoon, lower the eggs into the boiling water and cook for 6 to 7 minutes. Using the slotted spoon, transfer the eggs to the ice bath to stop the cooking. Let sit until cool enough to handle, then peel off the shells. Set aside.

To cook the sausages, in a large skillet over medium heat, warm the oil. Add the sausages and cook, turning occasionally, until browned and cooked through, about 10 minutes. Transfer to a cutting board, let rest for a few minutes, then thinly slice crosswise. Reserve the skillet.

To make the sauce, in a bowl, stir together the ketchup, gochujang, sugar, soy sauce, gochugaru, curry powder, garlic, and water until well mixed. Return the skillet to medium heat and add the sauce. Bring the mixture to a simmer and cook, stirring, until thickened, 2 to 3 minutes.

To assemble, drain the rice cakes if they were soaked. Add the rice cakes to the skillet with the sauce and cook, stirring occasionally, until the rice cakes are coated with the sauce and have softened, 5 to 7 minutes. Add the reserved sausages, stir to combine, and simmer until the sauce has thickened slightly, 1 to 2 minutes.

To serve, divide the mixture among four shallow bowls and garnish with the sesame seeds, scallions, and a sprinkle of curry powder. If using the eggs, halve them and rest, yolk-side up, on top of each bowl. Serve at once.

Nutrition Values (per serving): Energy (kJ) ~2176 kJ, Calories ~520 kcal, Fat ~24 g, Saturated Fat ~8 g, Carbohydrate ~58 g, Sugar ~10 g, Dietary Fiber ~2 g, Protein ~18 g, Cholesterol ~60 mg, Sodium ~1,200 mg

Cherry Balsamic Pork with Roasted Potatoes & Broccoli

Sweet, tangy, and irresistibly savory, this dish ranks in our Top 10 Hall of Fame recipes for good reason. Pork tenderloin is coated in a jammy cherry balsamic glaze that clings to every mouthful, while simply seasoned roasted broccoli and thyme-flecked potatoes provide an earthy backdrop. Loved by cooks and diners alike, the glaze delivers a perfect balance of fruitiness and acidity, making each bite memorable and the meal feel truly special.

MAKES 4 SERVINGS

1½ lb (680 g) fingerling potatoes, unpeeled, halved lengthwise

Olive oil, for drizzling

1 tsp dried thyme

Kosher salt and freshly ground pepper

1 lb (450 g) broccoli florets

1 pork tenderloin (about 1½ lb/680 g)

1 shallot, halved lengthwise and thinly sliced crosswise

3 Tbsp plus 1 tsp balsamic vinegar

2 Tbsp cherry preserves

2 Tbsp water

1 tsp sugar (optional)

2 Tbsp unsalted butter

Preheat the oven to 450°F (230°C).

To roast the potatoes, on a large sheet pan, toss the potatoes with a drizzle of oil, the thyme, and a pinch each of salt and pepper, coating evenly. Spread in a single layer. Roast for 10 minutes.

Prep the broccoli while the potatoes start roasting. In a medium bowl, toss the broccoli with a drizzle of oil and a pinch each of salt and pepper. After the potatoes have been roasting for 10 minutes, remove the sheet pan from the oven and toss the potatoes. Push them toward one side of the sheet pan. Spread the broccoli on the other side of the sheet pan. Return the vegetables to the oven and roast until the potatoes are crisp and tender and broccoli is tender and lightly crisped, 12 to 15 minutes longer.

While the vegetables are cooking, roast the pork. Season the pork all over with salt and pepper. In a large skillet over medium-high heat, warm a drizzle of oil. When the oil is shimmering, add the pork and cook, turning occasionally, until nicely browned all over, 6 to 8 minutes. Remove the skillet from the heat and transfer the pork to a small sheet pan. Reserve the skillet.

Roast the pork in the oven alongside the vegetables until cooked to your liking, 8 to 12 minutes. For a slightly pink center, roast until an instant-read thermometer inserted into the thickest part reads 140° to 145°F (60° to 63°C).

continued . . .

Cherry Balsamic Pork with Roasted Potatoes & Broccoli

continued from page 72 . . .

To make the sauce, return the skillet to medium heat and add a drizzle of oil. When the oil is shimmering, add the shallot and cook, stirring, until lightly browned, 4 to 5 minutes. Add the vinegar and bring to a simmer, stirring to scrape up any browned bits from the pan bottom. Continue to simmer, stirring occasionally, until reduced by half. Add the cherry preserves and water and stir well, then season with salt, pepper, and sugar (if using). Remove the skillet from the heat, add the butter, and stir until it melts. Set the glaze aside in the skillet until the pork is done roasting.

To glaze the pork, return the skillet to medium heat. Transfer the pork to the skillet and turn to coat in the glaze. Using tongs, transfer the pork to a cutting board, letting any excess glaze drip off into the skillet. Let the pork rest for 2 minutes, then cut into medallions.

To serve, divide the pork evenly among four plates and drizzle with the remaining glaze in the pan. Serve with the broccoli and potatoes.

Nutrition Values (per serving): Energy (kJ) 2385 kJ, Calories 570 kcal, Fat 21 g, Saturated Fat 7 g, Carbohydrate 52 g, Sugar 19 g, Dietary Fiber 8 g, Protein 39 g, Cholesterol 125 mg, Sodium 160 mg

“Because feeding people well means caring **for the world we share.”**

–Michelle

Braised Sausages with Sweet-and-Sour Red Cabbage

Flavorful sausages meet sweet-and-sour red cabbage in this hearty old-school meal. The cabbage is lightly braised with a sweet-tart apple and balsamic vinegar, creating a tangy-sweet side that pairs perfectly with pan-braised sausages infused with thyme and onions. Finished with a touch of mustard and a sprinkle of fresh parsley, this dish is both rustic and refined, ideal for a weeknight family dinner or a more leisurely weekend company meal.

MAKES 4 SERVINGS

SWEET-AND-SOUR RED CABBAGE

1 Tbsp unsalted butter or olive oil

½ head red cabbage (about 1½ lb/680 g), quartered, cored, and thinly shredded

1 sweet-tart, crisp apple, such as Honeycrisp or Pink Lady, cored, peeled, and shredded

Kosher salt

¼ cup (60 ml) balsamic vinegar

BRAISED SAUSAGES

1 Tbsp vegetable oil

4 large link sausages (about 1¼ lb/570 g), such as bratwurst or bangers

1 Tbsp unsalted butter

½ yellow onion, thinly sliced

1 fresh thyme sprig

Kosher salt and freshly ground pepper

½ cup (120 ml) beer or chicken broth

1 Tbsp whole-grain mustard

Chopped fresh flat-leaf parsley, for garnish

To make the cabbage, in a saucepan over medium heat, melt the butter. Add the cabbage and apple, season with salt, and cook, stirring, until the cabbage starts to wilt slightly, about 3 minutes. Add the vinegar, stir to combine, and bring to a boil. Turn down the heat to low, cover, and cook, stirring occasionally, until the cabbage is very tender, about 35 minutes. You want the cabbage to stay moist but not too watery, so if the cabbage starts to become too dry, add a little water.

To brown the sausages, while the cabbage cooks, in a skillet over medium heat, warm the oil. Add the sausages and cook, turning occasionally, until nicely browned all over, about 5 minutes. Transfer to a plate and set aside. The sausages will not be cooked through and will finish cooking later.

To cook the onion, with the skillet still over medium heat, add the butter, onion, and thyme and season well with salt and pepper. Cook, stirring occasionally, until the onion is golden brown, 6 to 7 minutes.

To braise the sausages, add the beer and mustard to the onion, stirring and scraping up any browned bits from the pan bottom. Return the sausages to the skillet and bring the mixture to a boil. Turn down the heat to low, cover partially, and simmer until the liquid reduces and the sausages are fully cooked, about 20 minutes.

To serve, pile the cabbage mixture onto four plates, dividing it evenly, then top each mound with a sausage. Spoon the onion sauce over the top, garnish with parsley, and serve right away.

Nutrition Values (per serving): Energy (kJ) ~2008 kJ, Calories ~480 kcal, Fat ~32 g, Saturated Fat ~11 g, Carbohydrate ~22 g, Sugar ~12 g, Dietary Fiber ~4 g, Protein ~20 g, Cholesterol ~75 mg, Sodium ~950 mg

BBQ Chicken Flatbread

Smoky, sweet, and just a little spicy, this flatbread bursts with robust flavors. Grilled chicken and melted smoked Cheddar mingle with fire-roasted corn, sweet caramelized onions, and pickled jalapeños for a bite that's both pleasing and playful. A drizzle of barbecue sauce and a sprinkle of fresh cilantro elevate each slice. For a zesty punch, substitute ¼ cup (30 g) pickled onions (page 79) for the caramelized onion. Take the pizza dough out of the refrigerator at least 1 hour or up to 3 hours in advance to bring it to room temperature.

MAKES 4 SERVINGS

1 Tbsp extra virgin olive oil

½ yellow onion, thinly sliced

Kosher salt and freshly ground pepper

¾ cup (110 g) shredded or chopped grilled chicken (page 38)

½ cup (140 g) favorite barbecue sauce

1 lb (450 g) purchased pizza dough, at room temperature

½ cup (60 g) shredded smoked or regular Cheddar cheese

¼ cup (35 g) frozen fire-roasted corn kernels, thawed

¼ cup (30 g) well-drained sliced pickled jalapeño chiles, roughly chopped

2 Tbsp chopped fresh cilantro

To make the caramelized onions, in a small skillet over medium heat, warm the oil. Add the onion and a pinch of salt and cook, stirring, until the onion is soft and golden brown, about 10 minutes. Set aside.

To prep the chicken, in a small bowl, toss together the chicken and 3 Tbsp of the barbecue sauce. Set aside.

Position an oven rack in the upper third of the oven and preheat the oven to 550°F (290°C) or as high as it will go. When it is fully preheated, and as you prep the flatbread, turn off the oven and turn on the broiler.

To prep the dough, lightly oil a large sheet pan. Put the dough on the prepared sheet pan and gently stretch it into a rectangle roughly 10 by 15 inches (25 by 38 cm). (If the dough doesn't want to stretch easily, let it rest for a few minutes before continuing.)

To assemble the flatbread, brush the dough evenly with 2 Tbsp of the barbecue sauce. Top with the reserved onion and chicken, then the cheese, corn, and jalapeños, spreading the ingredients evenly over the top of the dough. Drizzle with the remaining 3 Tbsp barbecue sauce.

To bake the flatbread, turn off the broiler and return the oven to 550°F (290°C). Slide the sheet pan onto the upper rack and bake the flatbread until the cheese is melted and the crust is browned and cooked through, about 10 minutes.

To serve, remove the flatbread from the oven, garnish with the cilantro, and cut into wedges.

Nutrition Values (per serving): Energy (kJ) ~2008 kJ, Calories ~480 kcal, Fat ~16 g, Saturated Fat ~6 g, Carbohydrate ~58 g, Sugar ~10 g, Dietary Fiber ~3 g, Protein ~22 g, Cholesterol ~55 mg, Sodium ~950 mg

Chicken Shawarma Naan Tacos

Here, Middle Eastern shawarma flavors are downsized into tasty cross-cultural tacos. Gently spiced chicken is topped with quick-pickled red onion for a zesty-sour punch and cucumber, cherry tomatoes, and cilantro for brightness and crunch. Soft, small naan breads hold all the elements together, while a spiced yogurt-harissa sauce provides the finishing touch. You can use boneless, skinless chicken thighs in place of the breasts, giving them a few extra minutes to cook.

MAKES 8 TACOS; 4 SERVINGS

PICKLED RED ONIONS

½ red onion, thinly sliced

1 cup (240 ml) boiling water

3 Tbsp rice vinegar

1 tsp sugar

Pinch of ground cumin

Pinch of kosher salt

CHICKEN SHAWARMA

1½ lb (680 g) boneless, skinless chicken breasts

2 Tbsp fresh lemon juice

2 Tbsp olive oil, plus more for cooking

2 Tbsp shawarma seasoning

2 garlic cloves, minced

½ cup (120 g) plain yogurt

2 Tbsp harissa sauce, plus more as needed

8 mini naan breads (about 5 inches/13 cm in diameter), toasted

1 cup (115 g) thinly sliced cucumber

1 cup (170 g) halved cherry or grape tomatoes (about 6 oz)

¼ cup (10 g) chopped fresh cilantro

To make the pickled onions, in a saucepan, combine the onion and boiling water. Let sit for 5 minutes, then drain and rinse well. Set the onion aside. Add the vinegar, sugar, cumin, and salt to the saucepan and bring to a boil over medium-high heat. Add the onion and stir to combine, then remove from the heat and set aside to cool. Transfer to an airtight container and refrigerate for 30 minutes or up to 2 weeks.

To prep the chicken, lay a chicken breast on a cutting board. Using the flat side of a meat mallet, gently pound the chicken to an even thickness of about ¾ inch (2 cm). Repeat with the remaining breasts.

To marinate the chicken, in a bowl, whisk together the lemon juice, oil, shawarma seasoning, and garlic. Add the chicken, turning it in the marinade to coat completely. Cover and refrigerate for at least 30 minutes or up 24 hours.

To cook the chicken, heat a large, heavy skillet over high heat, then drizzle the pan with enough oil to coat the bottom lightly. When the oil is shimmering, add the chicken and cook, turning occasionally and covering the pan about halfway through cooking, until the chicken is nicely browned on both sides and cooked through, about 10 minutes. Transfer to a cutting board and let rest for 5 minutes.

To make the yogurt sauce, in a bowl, stir together the yogurt and harissa sauce. Taste and add more harissa sauce if needed.

To serve, thinly slice the chicken across the grain and divide the chicken between the naan breads. Top with the pickled onions, cucumber, tomatoes, and cilantro, dividing them evenly. Drizzle with the yogurt sauce and serve.

Nutrition Values (per 2-taco serving): Energy (kJ) ~2176 kJ, Calories ~520 kcal, Fat ~20 g, Saturated Fat ~5 g, Carbohydrate ~50 g, Sugar ~6 g, Dietary Fiber ~3 g, Protein ~36 g, Cholesterol ~95 mg, Sodium ~780 mg

Orecchiette with Broccoli Rabe & Pancetta

Bitter, tender broccoli rabe meets salty pancetta and nutty Parmesan in this classic Italian pasta dish from our brand partner Colavita, the family-owned premium Italian specialty products company. Garlic, anchovies, and a hint of red pepper flakes add depth and complexity to the sauce, and orecchiette (little ears) pasta cradles every flavorful bite in this celebration of authentic Italian flavors.

MAKES 4 TO 6 SERVINGS

1 lb (450 g) broccoli rabe, tough ends trimmed

1 lb (450 g) orecchiette

3 Tbsp extra virgin olive oil, plus more for drizzling

2 oz (55 g) pancetta, diced

2 tsp minced garlic

2 olive oil–packed anchovy fillets

½ tsp red pepper flakes

1 Tbsp chopped fresh oregano leaves

1 cup (30 g) grated Parmesan cheese

Kosher salt and freshly ground black pepper

To blanch the broccoli rabe, fill a bowl with ice and water for an ice bath. Bring a large, wide saucepan of salted water to a boil over high heat. Add the broccoli rabe and cook until tender-crisp, about 2 minutes. Drain the broccoli rabe and plunge it into the ice bath until chilled, about 5 minutes. Drain well, transfer to a cutting board, and chop.

To cook the pasta, fill the saucepan with salted water and bring to a boil over high heat. Add the pasta, bring the water back to a boil, and cook, stirring occasionally, until just shy of al dente (about 1 minute before the desired doneness), about 7 minutes or according to package directions. Scoop out 1½ cups (360 ml) of the pasta water, then drain the pasta and set the reserved water and pasta aside separately.

To make the sauce, return the saucepan to the stovetop over medium heat. Add the oil and pancetta and cook, stirring, until it begins to color on the edges, 4 to 5 minutes. Add the garlic and anchovies and, using a spoon, mash the anchovies to break them up. Cook, stirring often, until the garlic is very aromatic and begins to color lightly, about 30 seconds, then add the red pepper flakes and stir well.

To finish the pasta, add the reserved broccoli rabe and pasta, half of the reserved pasta water, the oregano, and ½ cup (15 g) of the cheese. Season with salt and black pepper, then stir gently until all the ingredients are evenly mixed and heated through. Adjust the consistency of the sauce with additional pasta water as needed. Taste and adjust the seasoning with salt and black pepper if needed.

To serve, divide the pasta among individual plates. Garnish with the remaining Parmesan, dividing it evenly, and a drizzle of oil and serve.

Nutrition Values (per serving for 6 servings): Energy (kJ) ~1925 kJ, Calories ~460 kcal, Fat ~16 g, Saturated Fat ~4 g, Carbohydrate ~58 g, Sugar ~3 g, Dietary Fiber ~5 g, Protein ~18 g, Cholesterol ~20 mg, Sodium ~620 mg

Regent Sherwood
JAPAN

Chicken Saltimbocca Caprese

Chicken saltimbocca gets a fresh, summery twist with the addition of a deconstructed caprese salad. Chicken breasts are quickly cooked in oil and butter and a splash of white wine and then topped with basil leaves, prosciutto, and mozzarella and finished with garlicky blistered cherry tomatoes. Garnished with a sprinkle of chopped basil, this dish delivers a harmonious balance of savory, creamy, and fresh flavors.

MAKES 4 SERVINGS

2 large boneless, skinless chicken breasts (about 1½ lb/680 g)

Kosher salt and freshly ground pepper

Extra virgin olive oil, for drizzling

1 lb (450 g) cherry or grape tomatoes

1 garlic clove, minced

2 Tbsp unsalted butter

2 Tbsp dry white wine

8 large fresh basil leaves, plus 1 Tbsp chopped, for garnish

4 thin slices prosciutto

1 (8-oz/225-g) ball fresh mozzarella cheese, cut into 8 slices

To prep the chicken, lay a chicken breast on a cutting board. Using the flat side of a meat mallet (or the bottom of a small, heavy skillet), gently pound the chicken to an even thickness of about ½ inch (12 mm). Cut the breast into two equal pieces. Repeat with the second chicken breast. Transfer the four pieces to a medium plate. Season generously all over with salt and pepper, then drizzle on both sides with oil. Set aside at room temperature while you make the tomatoes.

To blister the tomatoes, position an oven rack about 4 inches (10 cm) under the broiler and preheat the broiler. In a large broiler-proof skillet, toss together the tomatoes and garlic with a drizzle of oil. Season with salt and pepper. Slide the skillet under the broiler and broil until the tomatoes begin to blister and soften, about 7 minutes. Transfer the tomatoes to a plate. Leave the broiler on.

To sear the chicken, place the same skillet over medium heat and add 1 Tbsp oil and the butter. When the butter has melted, swirl the pan to coat the bottom, then add the chicken in a single layer. Sear the chicken until nicely browned on the underside, about 4 minutes. Flip the chicken, add the wine, and continue to cook until nearly cooked through, about 4 minutes longer.

To finish the chicken, top each piece with two basil leaves, one prosciutto slice, and two mozzarella slices. Place the skillet under the broiler until the cheese is melted, about 2 minutes.

To serve, transfer the chicken to four plates. Top with the blistered tomatoes and a sprinkle of basil and serve right away.

Nutrition Values (per serving): Energy (kJ) ~2008 kJ, Calories ~480 kcal, Fat ~28 g, Saturated Fat ~10 g, Carbohydrate ~8 g, Sugar ~4 g, Dietary Fiber ~2 g, Protein ~46 g, Cholesterol ~145 mg, Sodium ~780 mg

Red Curry Chicken Noodles with Green Beans

In this Southeast Asian–inspired supper, succulent chicken thighs and crisp green beans swim in a creamy red curry sauce brightened with lime, cilantro, and scallions. Red curry paste packs bold heat, which is tempered by the silky, balanced richness of coconut milk and a touch of brown sugar. Tossed with springy Chinese noodles or ramen, this hearty curry delivers a heady mix of spice, sweetness, and umami. If you have makrut lime leaves on hand, add a couple of leaves to the simmering chicken for a citrusy, floral accent.

MAKES 4 SERVINGS

1 (13.5–fl oz/405-ml) can coconut milk, well shaken

½ small yellow onion, coarsely chopped

¼ cup (10 g) chopped fresh cilantro, plus more for garnish

2 garlic cloves, chopped

Finely grated zest and juice of 1 lime

2 Tbsp red curry paste

2 Tbsp Asian fish sauce

1 Tbsp packed light brown sugar

4 large boneless, skinless chicken thighs (about 1 lb/450 g)

1½ cups (170 g) frozen cut green beans

3 scallions, white and green parts, thinly sliced

1 lb (450 g) fresh Chinese wheat noodles, or 8 oz (225 g) dried ramen noodles

To make the sauce, in a blender, combine the coconut milk, yellow onion, cilantro, garlic, lime zest and juice, curry paste, fish sauce, and brown sugar and blend on medium-high speed until smooth.

To simmer the chicken, put the chicken thighs into a medium saucepan and pour in the sauce. Bring to a boil over medium-high heat, then turn down the heat to low, cover partially, and simmer, stirring every so often, until the chicken is cooked through and very tender, about 30 minutes.

To finish the sauce, using tongs, transfer the chicken to a cutting board and let cool slightly. Meanwhile, add the green beans and scallions to the saucepan and stir to mix. Bring to a simmer over medium heat, cover, and cook until the green beans are tender, about 4 minutes.

While the green beans cook, chop the chicken into bite-size pieces. When the green beans are ready, return the chicken to the pan and stir to heat through. Cover and keep warm over low heat.

To cook the noodles, bring a large saucepan three-fourths full of salted water to a boil over high heat. Add the noodles and cook according to the package directions. Drain.

To serve, divide the noodles among four bowls. Ladle the chicken curry over the noodles, garnish with cilantro, and serve at once.

Nutrition Values (per serving): Energy (kJ) ~2343 kJ, Calories ~560 kcal, Fat ~24 g, Saturated Fat ~12 g, Carbohydrate ~55 g, Sugar ~8 g, Dietary Fiber ~4 g, Protein ~32 g, Cholesterol ~95 mg, Sodium ~980 mg

Skillet Suppers 3

"One-pan cooking has always lived at the intersection of comfort & creativity."

—Courtney Roker Laga, HelloFresh Test Kitchen

There is a kind of quiet magic that happens when everything—your ingredients, your memories, your instincts—comes together in a single pan. Maybe it's the simplicity, maybe it's the efficiency, or maybe it's the way a well-seasoned skillet can feel like an extension of your own hands.

No matter how many fun kitchen pots or pans I find to cook with, I always come back to the skillet. And as a home cook, mom, and foodie, I love it primarily because it connects me to the people and flavors that shaped me. My mother's cast-iron skillet stayed permanently on the stove, its surface carrying the imprint of every meal she made. It held the scent of Saturday-morning pancakes, the sizzle of weeknight chicken, and the warmth of foods seasoned not just with salt but with stories.

This chapter celebrates that kind of cooking, the kind that feels familiar, deeply personal, and wonderfully adaptable. One-pan recipes are an invitation to take the flavors you grew up with, the ones that speak to your heritage, and give them room to shine. They push you to pull out the handwritten recipe card that lived in your abuela's kitchen drawer and ask yourself, what would this look like in a skillet? They nudge you to try that spice blend you love or the ingredient that reminds you of home and let it transform something simple into something meaningful.

One-pan meals are also forgiving. You can improvise, play, swap ingredients, and trust your senses. The heat, the aroma, the sound of a good sizzle—they all speak to you if you listen. And before you know it, you've created something both new and familiar, something undeniably yours.

My hope is that these recipes become starting points, not finish lines—that they inspire you to stir in your own stories, your family traditions, your cultural roots, and the flavors that make you feel most at home. Because a skillet doesn't have to be just a pan. It can be a place where heritage meets everyday life, where dinner becomes memory, and where your cooking truly becomes you. Here's to one pan, endless possibilities and meals that carry meaning.

—Michelle

Veggie Chili Tamale Pie

Hearty, colorful, and packed with flavor, this chili tamale pie is a two-in-one comfort feast. A savory chili of beans, tomatoes, corn, and spices is topped with a golden crown of cheese-rich corn bread. Serve with dollops of sour cream, hot pepper sauce, and chopped fresh cilantro.

MAKES 6 TO 8 SERVINGS

VEGGIE CHILI

1 Tbsp vegetable oil

1 small yellow onion, chopped

1 small red bell pepper, seeded and finely chopped

1 medium carrot, finely chopped

Kosher salt and freshly ground black pepper

2 Tbsp mild chili powder

2 tsp ground cumin

1 (15-oz/430-g) can *each* pinto beans, black beans, red kidney beans, and garbanzo beans, drained and rinsed

1 (15-oz/430-g) can crushed tomatoes

1 (4-oz/115-g) can diced green chiles

½ cup (120 ml) water

½ cup (65 g) corn kernels

CORN BREAD TOPPING

½ cup (70 g) cornmeal

½ cup (70 g) all-purpose flour

2 Tbsp sugar

1½ tsp baking powder

½ tsp kosher salt

½ cup (65 g) packed shredded Cheddar cheese

½ cup (120 ml) whole milk

1 large egg

2 Tbsp vegetable oil

To make the veggie chili, in a deep, heavy 10-inch (25-cm) ovenproof skillet over medium heat, warm the oil. Add the onion, red bell pepper, carrot, and a big pinch of salt and cook, stirring occasionally, until the vegetables are tender and starting to brown, about 9 minutes. Stir in the chili powder and cumin until well mixed and fragrant, about 30 seconds. Add all the beans, the tomatoes, green chiles, and water, stir well, and bring to a boil, stirring occasionally. Turn down the heat to low, cover partially, and simmer until thickened and fragrant, about 45 minutes. Stir in the corn kernels during the last 15 minutes. If the chili gets too thick or begins to stick, add a little water.

Preheat the oven to 425°F (220°C).

To make the corn bread topping, in a medium bowl, whisk together the cornmeal, flour, sugar, baking powder, and salt. Stir in the cheese. In a small bowl, whisk together the milk, egg, and oil. Add the milk mixture to the cornmeal mixture and stir to combine. Pour the cornbread batter over the veggie chili in an even layer, spreading it gently to smooth it out.

Bake until the filling is bubbly and the corn bread is cooked through and a toothpick inserted in the middle comes out clean, about 18 minutes.

To serve, place the skillet in the center of the table. Set the sour cream, hot pepper sauce, and cilantro alongside, if using. Invite everyone to help themselves.

Nutrition Values (per serving for 8 servings): Energy (kJ) ~1757 kJ, Calories ~420 kcal, Fat ~14 g, Saturated Fat ~5 g, Carbohydrate ~60 g, Sugar ~10 g, Dietary Fiber ~11 g, Protein ~14 g, Cholesterol ~35 mg, Sodium ~780 mg

Apple Cider Chicken with Butternut Squash

This dish captures the cozy flavors of autumn, pairing crisp-skinned chicken thighs with sweet, tender roasted butternut squash and tart apple slices. Red onion and fresh rosemary add savory depth, a touch of honey delivers added sweetness, and apple cider and grainy mustard create a flavorful pan sauce. If you like, swap in another winter squash variety, such as Red Kuri or kabocha, or even a Sugar Pie pumpkin for the butternut squash.

MAKES 4 SERVINGS

- 2 cups (240 g) peeled, cubed butternut squash, in ¾-inch (2-cm) cubes
- 1 sweet-tart, crisp apple, such as Honeycrisp or Pink Lady, halved, cored, and cut into slices ¼ inch (6 mm) thick
- ¼ small red onion, thinly sliced
- 1 Tbsp chopped fresh rosemary leaves
- Kosher salt and freshly ground pepper
- Olive oil, for drizzling
- 4 large bone-in, skin-on chicken thighs (about 1½ lb/680 g)
- ¾ cup (175 ml) apple cider
- 2 Tbsp whole-grain mustard
- 1 Tbsp honey
- 2 Tbsp unsalted butter, cut into chunks
- Chopped fresh flat-leaf parsley, for garnish (optional)

Preheat the oven to 425°F (220°C).

To prep the squash and apple, in a medium bowl, toss together the butternut squash, apple, onion, and rosemary. Season with salt and pepper, drizzle with a little oil, and toss until the squash and apple are evenly coated. Set aside.

To brown the chicken, pat the chicken dry with paper towels, then season generously all over with salt and pepper. Heat a 12-inch (30-cm) ovenproof skillet over medium heat. When the pan is hot, add the chicken, skin-side down, and sear, without turning, until the skin is crisp and golden brown, 6 to 8 minutes. Turn and lightly brown the second side, about 5 minutes (the chicken will finish cooking in the oven). Transfer to a large plate.

To make the glaze, with the skillet still over medium heat, add the cider, mustard, and honey and bring to a simmer, stirring. Cook, stirring occasionally, until the mixture reduces slightly, about 2 minutes. Add the butter, and when it melts, whisk to combine.

To finish the dish, return the chicken thighs to the skillet and turn them to coat evenly in the glaze. Arrange them skin-side up in a single layer, then scatter the butternut squash mixture evenly around the chicken. Transfer the skillet to the oven.

Roast, uncovered and stirring the squash a few times, until the chicken is cooked through and the squash is tender, about 35 minutes. The chicken is ready when an instant-read thermometer inserted into the thickest part of a thigh registers 165°F (74°C). Remove from the oven, garnish with parsley (if using), and serve at once.

Nutrition Values (per serving): Energy (kJ) ~2150 kJ, Calories ~515 kcal, Fat ~34 g, Saturated Fat ~11 g, Carbohydrate ~20 g, Sugar ~13 g, Dietary Fiber ~3 g, Protein ~29 g, Cholesterol ~155 mg, Sodium ~620 mg

French Onion Pasta Bake

Pasta goes straight from the package into this rich French onion soup–inspired sauce, soaking up every bit of flavor as it cooks. Sweet caramelized onions, plenty of earthy cremini mushrooms, and a splash of wine mingle with thyme and Worcestershire sauce, creating a deeply savory base. Finished with cream and bubbling Gruyère, this showstopper is packed with flavor and dangerously indulgent.

MAKES 4 SERVINGS

- 2 Tbsp unsalted butter
- 1 large yellow onion, halved and thinly sliced
- Kosher salt and freshly ground pepper
- 8 oz (225 g) cremini mushrooms, sliced
- 2 fresh thyme sprigs
- ¼ cup (60 ml) dry white wine
- 2 Tbsp sherry wine
- 8 oz (225 g) ziti, short rigatoni, penne, or orecchiette
- 2 cups (475 ml) beef, chicken, or mushroom broth
- 1 Tbsp Worcestershire sauce
- 2 Tbsp heavy cream
- 1½ cups (170 g) grated Gruyère cheese

To caramelize the onions, in a deep, heavy 10-inch broiler-proof skillet over medium heat, melt the butter. Add the onion, season well with salt, and toss to combine. Cover and cook, stirring occasionally, until the onion browns and caramelizes, about 18 minutes. If the onion starts to brown too quickly, lower the heat.

Position one oven rack in the middle and one in the upper third of the oven and preheat the oven to 400°F (200°C).

To cook the mushrooms, uncover the skillet and add the mushrooms and thyme. Continue to cook, stirring often, until the mushrooms start to become tender, about 4 minutes. Add the white wine and sherry and stir to mix, scraping up any browned bits from the pan bottom.

To cook the pasta, add the pasta, broth, and Worcestershire sauce to the skillet and stir to mix well. Increase the heat to medium-high and bring to a boil. Cover the skillet with aluminum foil and then the lid and transfer the skillet to the middle rack of the oven. Bake, stirring every 10 minutes or so, until the pasta is tender to your liking, 35 to 40 minutes. (If the pasta starts to dry out, add a little boiling water.)

To finish, remove the skillet from the oven. Turn on the broiler. Remove the lid and foil and pick out and discard the thyme sprigs. Stir in the cream, mixing well, then top evenly with the cheese. Slide the skillet onto the top rack under the broiler and broil until the cheese is melted and browned, about 4 minutes. Serve directly from the skillet.

Nutrition Values (per serving): Energy (kJ) ~2176 kJ, Calories ~520 kcal, Fat ~22 g, Saturated Fat ~13 g, Carbohydrate ~58 g, Sugar ~6 g, Dietary Fiber ~4 g, Protein ~20 g, Cholesterol ~65 mg, Sodium ~780 mg

Spanish Tortilla

This classic Spanish recipe from Ana Garcia, part of the founding team of Meals with Meaning, has been enjoyed by her family and friends for years. The humble mix of eggs and potatoes is a tradition that shines whether served warm for brunch or at room temperature for gatherings. Flipping takes practice, but even imperfect turns taste delicious. Serve it like Ana does, with Kewpie mayo, thinly sliced jamón ibérico, and a glass of Rioja.

MAKES 6 SERVINGS

3 lb (1.4 kg) Yukon Gold potatoes, peeled, quartered lengthwise, then cut crosswise into ⅛-inch (3 mm) slices

½ cup (120 ml) extra virgin olive oil, plus more if needed

Kosher salt

10 large eggs

To cook the potatoes, in a 12-inch (30-cm) nonstick skillet over medium heat, warm the oil. Add one-third of the potatoes, then season with salt. Stir gently to coat the potatoes in oil. Turn down the heat to medium-low, cover the skillet, and cook, stirring occasionally, until the potatoes are tender but not browned, 12 to 15 minutes.

Using a slotted spoon, transfer the potatoes to a large bowl, letting excess oil drip back into the skillet. Repeat to cook the remaining potatoes in two more batches. When all the potatoes are cooked, pour the oil into a small heatproof bowl and set aside. Reserve the skillet.

In a bowl, whisk the eggs with 1 tsp salt until blended.

To cook the tortilla, place the skillet over medium heat and drizzle a few Tbsp of the reserved oil onto the bottom. Transfer the potatoes to the skillet, using a spatula to pack the mixture into a flat "cake" about 2 inches (5 cm) thick. Pour the egg mixture over the potatoes, shaking the pan to remove any air pockets. Cook, running the spatula around the edges to prevent sticking, until the bottom of the tortilla is golden brown and the center begins to set, 5 to 6 minutes.

To flip and finish the tortilla, turn off the heat. Invert a flat serving plate that is slightly larger than the skillet over the skillet. Using a quick motion, invert the plate and pan together, releasing the tortilla onto the plate. Slide the tortilla, browned-side up, back into the skillet. Place over medium heat and cook until the eggs are set but still a little creamy, 3 to 4 minutes.

To serve, slide the tortilla onto a serving plate and let rest for 10 to 15 minutes before slicing. Serve warm or at room temperature.

Nutrition Values (per serving): Energy (kJ) ~1506 kJ, Calories ~360 kcal, Fat ~22 g, Saturated Fat ~4 g, Carbohydrate ~24 g, Sugar ~ 2 g, Dietary Fiber ~2 g, Protein ~12 g, Cholesterol ~190 mg, Sodium ~400 mg

Layered Chicken Enchilada Casserole

Layered like a skillet lasagna, this casserole transforms all the zesty flavors of classic enchiladas into a quick weeknight-friendly dish. Tender shredded chicken, sautéed bell peppers and onions, and a lightly spiced tomato-chile sauce are sandwiched between corn tortillas and topped with melted cheese. A squeeze of lime and a sprinkle of cilantro brighten each serving. If you like, serve with shredded cabbage or romaine on top for a refreshing crunch.

MAKES 4 TO 6 SERVINGS

2 limes

2 cups (285 g) shredded cooked chicken (page 38)

1 tsp plus 1 Tbsp chili powder

Kosher salt and freshly ground black pepper

2 Tbsp unsalted butter

½ medium yellow onion, finely chopped

1 small red bell pepper, seeded and finely chopped

2 Tbsp all-purpose flour

1 tsp cumin

1 cup (240 ml) chicken broth

1 cup (260 g) canned crushed tomatoes

1 (4-oz/115-g) can mild diced green chiles

⅓ cup (45 g) fresh or frozen corn kernels

¼ cup (60 g) sour cream, plus more for serving

¼ cup (10 g) chopped fresh cilantro, plus more for serving

Vegetable oil, for brushing

8 (6-inch/15-cm) corn tortillas

1¼ cups (140 g) shredded Monterey Jack and/or Cheddar cheese

To season the chicken, finely grate the zest from 1 lime into a medium bowl. Cut the lime in half and squeeze the juice from half of the lime into the bowl. Add the chicken, 1 tsp of the chili powder, and ½ tsp salt and toss to coat the chicken evenly. Set aside.

To make the sauce, in a 10-inch (25-cm) cast-iron or other heavy ovenproof skillet over medium heat, melt the butter. Add the onion, bell pepper, and a pinch of salt and cook, stirring occasionally, until the vegetables have softened and are starting to brown, about 7 minutes. Turn down the heat to medium-low, stir in the flour, cumin, and the remaining 1 Tbsp chili powder, and cook, stirring, for 1 minute longer.

Increase the heat to medium, pour in the broth, and stir until the mixture is smooth and slightly thickened, about 2 minutes. Stir in the tomatoes and green chiles and bring to a gentle boil, then turn down the heat to low, cover partially, and simmer, stirring occasionally, until fragrant, about 10 minutes.

Add the reserved chicken, corn kernels, sour cream, the juice from the remaining ½ lime, and the cilantro and stir to combine. Season with salt and pepper. Transfer the mixture to a bowl and clean the skillet.

Preheat the oven to 350°F (175°C).

To soften the tortillas, brush the skillet with oil and place over medium heat. When the skillet is hot, add a tortilla and warm, turning once, until soft and pliable. Transfer to a medium plate, then brush the skillet with more oil before adding the next tortilla. (If the pan gets too hot, lower the heat slightly.) Repeat until all the tortillas are softened, stacking them as they are ready, then cut the stack in half.

To assemble the casserole, ladle one-third of the chicken mixture into the skillet. Layer half of the tortillas over the chicken, overlapping them as needed to fit in the skillet. Add half of the remaining chicken mixture and top evenly with half of the cheese. Layer the remaining tortillas over the cheese, then top with the remaining chicken and finish with the remaining cheese.

Bake, uncovered, until hot and bubbling and the cheese is melted and browned, about 30 minutes. Remove from the oven.

To serve, cut the remaining lime into wedges. Garnish the casserole with cilantro and serve with sour cream and the lime wedges.

Nutrition Values (per serving for 6 servings): Energy (kJ) ~2000 kJ, Calories ~480 kcal, Fat ~20 g, Saturated Fat ~9 g, Carbohydrate ~42 g, Sugar ~ 6 g, Dietary Fiber ~5 g, Protein ~32 g, Cholesterol ~85 mg, Sodium ~780 mg

"Food is love & everyone deserves both."

–Marina Schulze, HelloFresh Test Kitchen

Za'atar Chicken & Potato Skillet

In this skillet dinner, crispy, golden chicken thighs sit atop tender, creamy potatoes, all infused with the earthy, citrusy warmth of za'atar, the versatile spice blend found throughout the Middle East. Red onion and garlic add depth, while pomegranate molasses, fresh lemon juice, and honey create a tart-sweet glaze. Finished with a sprinkle of fresh parsley and jewel-like pomegranate seeds, this dish delivers a wealth of savory, sweet, and bright flavors.

MAKES 4 SERVINGS

4 large bone-in, skin-on chicken thighs (about 1½ lb/680 g)

Kosher salt and freshly ground pepper

1 Tbsp plus 2 tsp za'atar

1½ lb (680 g) small Yukon Gold, fingerling, or other yellow potatoes, unpeeled, cut into 1-inch (2.5-cm) chunks

½ small red onion, halved and thinly sliced

3 garlic cloves, thinly sliced

Olive oil, for cooking

¼ cup (80 g) pomegranate molasses

2 Tbsp dry white wine or chicken broth

2 Tbsp fresh lemon juice

2 tsp honey

Chopped fresh flat-leaf parsley and pomegranate seeds, for garnish (optional)

Preheat the oven to 400°F (200°C).

To season the chicken, pat the chicken thighs dry with paper towels, then season all over with salt, pepper, and 1 Tbsp of the za'atar, rubbing some of the spices under the skin.

To brown the chicken, arrange the thighs, skin-side down, in a heavy, large ovenproof skillet and place over medium heat. Brown the chicken on the skin side, without turning, until nicely golden brown, 6 to 8 minutes. Turn and lightly brown the second side, about 5 minutes (the chicken will finish cooking in the oven). Transfer the chicken to a large plate.

Remove the skillet from over the heat. Add the potatoes, onion, and garlic to the skillet, drizzle with a little oil, then season generously with salt and pepper. Toss to combine.

To make the glaze, in a small microwave-safe bowl, combine the pomegranate molasses, wine, lemon juice, honey, and the remaining 2 tsp za'atar. Microwave the mixture for 10 to 20 seconds to loosen the honey, then whisk to mix well.

Brush the chicken thighs all over with the pomegranate molasses mixture, then top the potato mixture with the chicken thighs, skin-side up. Pour the remaining pomegranate molasses mixture over the top of the chicken so it drips down onto the potato mixture.

To bake, transfer the skillet to the oven and bake uncovered, stirring the potatoes once or twice during cooking, until the chicken is cooked through and the potatoes are tender, about 40 minutes. Serve at once.

Nutrition Values (per serving): Energy (kJ) ~2259 kJ, Calories ~540 kcal, Fat ~26 g, Saturated Fat ~6 g, Carbohydrate ~38 g, Sugar ~10 g, Dietary Fiber ~4 g, Protein ~36 g, Cholesterol ~145 mg, Sodium ~780 mg

Crispy Chicken & Chorizo Paella

Crisp-skinned chicken and smoky chorizo mingle with saffron-infused rice in this one-pan Spanish feast. Both impressive and approachable, paella is easily tailored to your favorite ingredients: omit the sausage and top the rice with grilled shrimp instead of chicken, or make it plant friendly with a medley of grilled or roasted vegetables and vegetable broth. You can easily turn it into six servings by using six chicken thighs.

MAKES 4 SERVINGS

4 large bone-in, skin-on chicken thighs (about 1½ lb/680 g)

Kosher salt and freshly ground black pepper

Extra virgin olive oil, for cooking

4 oz (115 g) Spanish chorizo, skin removed and cut crosswise into slices ¼ inch (6 mm) thick

1 small yellow onion, finely chopped

1 cup (200 g) short- or medium-grain paella rice, preferably Bomba variety

2 garlic cloves, minced

Large pinch of saffron threads bloomed in 2 Tbsp hot water

1 cup (180 g) diced tomatoes, with juices

1½ tsp smoked paprika

2 cups (475 ml) chicken broth, plus more if needed

1 (6-oz/170-g) jar roasted sweet red peppers, preferably Pimentón de la Vera, drained and cut into strips

⅔ cup (90 g) frozen petite peas

1 large lemon, cut into 4 wedges

To brown the chicken, season the thighs all over with salt and pepper. Arrange them, skin side down, in a heavy 10-inch (25-cm) ovenproof skillet and place over medium-high heat. Brown the chicken without turning, until the skin is crisp and golden, 6 to 8 minutes. Turn and brown the second side, about 5 minutes (the chicken will finish cooking in the oven). Transfer the chicken to a plate and pour off all but 1 Tbsp of the fat from the skillet. If there is not enough fat, add a little oil.

To cook the chorizo, turn down the heat to medium, add the chorizo, and cook, stirring, until lightly browned, about 2 minutes. Using a slotted spoon, transfer the chorizo to the plate holding the chicken. Leave the oil in the skillet.

Preheat the oven to 400°F (200°C). Add the onion to the skillet and cook, stirring, until it starts to brown and soften, about 5 minutes. Add the rice and cook, stirring, until toasted, about 3 minutes. Add the garlic and cook, stirring, for 1 minute. Add the saffron mixture, tomatoes, and paprika and cook, stirring, until the juices are bubbling. Pour in the broth, season with salt and pepper, and stir to mix. Bring to a boil.

Transfer the skillet to the oven and bake, uncovered, for 10 minutes, then nestle the chorizo and chicken thighs into the rice. Cover with aluminum foil and a lid, return to the oven, and bake for another 20 minutes. Uncover the skillet and sprinkle the red peppers and peas over the rice, pushing them into the rice and under the chicken so they are evenly distributed. Increase the oven temperature to 425°F (220°C). Return the skillet to the oven and bake, uncovered, until the liquid is absorbed and the rice and peas are tender, 10 to 13 minutes longer.

Let sit for 5 minutes, then serve with the lemon wedges.

Nutrition Values (per serving): Energy (kJ) ~2594 kJ, Calories ~620 kcal, Fat ~28 g, Saturated Fat ~8 g, Carbohydrate ~48 g, Sugar ~4 g, Dietary Fiber ~3 g, Protein ~38 g, Cholesterol ~145 mg, Sodium ~980 mg

SUR LA TABLE

Veggie Potpie with Biscuits

Here, a creamy, thyme-scented vegetable filling packed with broccoli, carrots, leeks, mushrooms, and sweet peas is topped with golden, flaky biscuits that crisp perfectly in the oven. Want chicken potpie? Just omit the broccoli and add 2½ cups (360 g) shredded or chopped cooked chicken (page 38) to the mixture after you make the filling and before you top it with the biscuits.

MAKES 6 SERVINGS

POTPIE FILLING

4 Tbsp (55 g) unsalted butter

1 (12-oz/340-g) broccoli crown, cut into small florets

2 medium carrots, diced

1 large leek, white and tender green parts, quartered lengthwise, and sliced crosswise

8 oz (225) cremini or button mushrooms, trimmed and sliced

1 tsp minced fresh thyme leaves, or ½ tsp dried thyme

Kosher salt and freshly ground pepper

¼ cup (35 g) all-purpose flour

2¼ cups (530 ml) vegetable or chicken broth, plus more if needed

¾ cup (175 ml) whole milk

½ cup (65 g) frozen peas

BISCUIT TOPPING

2 cups (280 g) all-purpose flour

2 tsp baking powder

½ tsp baking soda

½ tsp kosher salt

¾ cup (175 ml) buttermilk

6 Tbsp (85 g) unsalted butter, melted

To make the filling, in a 12-inch (30-cm) ovenproof skillet over medium heat, melt the butter. Add the broccoli, carrots, leek, mushrooms, and thyme and season generously with salt. Cook, stirring occasionally, until the vegetables release their liquid and start to become tender (they will continue cooking in the oven), about 7 minutes.

Sprinkle the flour over the vegetables and then stir until evenly coated. Slowly add the broth while stirring constantly, continuing to stir until smooth. Add the milk and peas and stir until well mixed. Bring to a gentle boil and cook, stirring occasionally, until slightly thickened (you want it to be fairly soupy, as it will continue to thicken in the oven), about 5 minutes. Season with salt and pepper. Remove from the heat and set aside.

Preheat the oven to 400°F (200°C).

To make the biscuit dough, in a medium bowl, stir together the flour, baking powder, baking soda, and salt. Add the buttermilk and butter and stir gently just until the flour mixture is fully moistened and the ingredients are well blended. Do not overmix. Drop 2-Tbsp-size portions of the dough onto the filling (a large cookie scoop works well here), spacing them evenly apart.

Bake until the biscuits are golden brown and cooked through and the filling is bubbling, 25 to 30 minutes. Let cool on a wire rack for about 10 minutes before serving.

Nutrition Values (per serving): Energy (kJ) ~1715 kJ, Calories ~410 kcal, Fat ~20 g, Saturated Fat ~12 g, Carbohydrate ~46 g, Sugar ~7 g, Dietary Fiber ~4 g, Protein ~9 g, Cholesterol ~55 mg, Sodium ~780 mg

Creamy Gnocchi, Bacon & Spinach Skillet

This is our take on the "marry me" recipe craze: gnocchi so creamy and appealing it might just inspire a proposal. Crispy bacon adds a smoky fragrance, sun-dried tomatoes bring tangy bursts of flavor, and a garlicky, slightly spicy tomato-cream sauce ties everything together. Baby spinach contributes color and melts into the sumptuous sauce which is guaranteed to have everyone swooning.

MAKES 4 SERVINGS

3 slices thick-cut bacon, cut crosswise into ½-inch (12-mm) pieces

2 Tbsp extra virgin olive oil

⅓ cup (35 g) drained, chopped sun-dried tomatoes in oil

3 garlic cloves, finely chopped

1 Tbsp tomato paste

½ tsp Italian seasoning

½ tsp red pepper flakes

1 Tbsp unsalted butter

1 (1 lb/450 g) package potato gnocchi

1¼ cups (300 ml) vegetable or chicken broth, plus more if needed

3 cups (80 g) firmly packed chopped baby spinach

¼ cup (60 ml) heavy cream

¼ cup (8 g) grated Parmesan cheese, plus more for serving

Kosher salt and freshly ground black pepper

3 Tbsp chopped fresh basil

To cook the sauce, in a large skillet over medium-low heat, cook the bacon, stirring occasionally, until just crisp, about 8 minutes. Pour off all but 1 Tbsp of the fat. Add 1 Tbsp of the oil, swirl the pan to coat the bottom, and then add the sun-dried tomatoes and garlic. Cook, stirring occasionally, until just starting to brown, 2 to 3 minutes. Add the tomato paste, Italian seasoning, and red pepper flakes and cook, stirring, until fragrant, about 1 minute. Transfer the tomato mixture to a small bowl.

To brown the gnocchi, add the remaining 1 Tbsp oil and the butter to the skillet and increase the heat to medium. When the butter melts, add the gnocchi and stir to coat, then spread in a single layer. Cook, without stirring, until they start to brown, about 3 minutes. Add the reserved sun-dried tomato mixture, then pour in the broth, stir until well mixed, and bring to a simmer. Turn down the heat to low and cook, stirring occasionally, until the gnocchi are tender and sauce is slightly reduced, about 3 minutes.

To finish the dish, stir in the spinach, cream, and Parmesan. Bring the mixture back to a simmer and cook, stirring gently, until the spinach is wilted and the cream and Parmesan are incorporated and heated through. Loosen the sauce with a little more broth if needed. Taste and adjust the seasoning with salt and black pepper if needed. Garnish with more Parmesan and with the basil and serve at once.

Nutrition Values (per serving): Energy (kJ) ~2176 kJ, Calories ~520 kcal, Fat ~26 g, Saturated Fat ~10 g, Carbohydrate ~52 g, Sugar ~4 g, Dietary Fiber ~4 g, Protein ~14 g, Cholesterol ~45 mg, Sodium ~780 mg

Lemony Chicken & Rice Skillet

Forget the decades-old casserole that called for condensed cream of chicken soup, cooked chicken, and rice. This chicken and rice skillet supper is bright, fresh, and full of flavor and goes together just as quickly as its old-school cousin. Here, chicken thighs are seared to golden perfection and lemon slices are caramelized slightly in the hot pan, infusing the dish with intense citrusy notes before being baked atop fragrant jasmine rice. The garnish of chopped green olives is optional but encouraged, as it adds a bright, briny finish.

MAKES 4 SERVINGS

4 large boneless, skinless chicken thighs (about 1 lb/450 g)

Kosher salt and freshly ground pepper

1 Tbsp olive oil

8 thin slices of lemon, seeded

3 Tbsp unsalted butter

2 Tbsp dry white wine

1 shallot, finely chopped

2 garlic cloves, minced

1 cup (200 g) jasmine rice

1⅓ cups (315 ml) chicken broth

3 Tbsp fresh lemon juice

¼ cup (45 g) chopped pitted green olives, such as Castelvetrano

Chopped fresh flat-leaf parsley, for garnish

To brown the chicken, pat the chicken dry with paper towels, then season generously all over with salt and pepper. In a heavy 10-inch skillet over medium-high heat, warm the oil. When the oil is shimmering, add the chicken, skinned-side down, in a single layer and sear until nicely browned, 6 to 7 minutes. Turn and sear until lightly browned on the second side, about 2 minutes (the chicken will finish cooking with the rice). Transfer the chicken to a large plate.

Add the lemon slices to the hot pan and sear, without turning, until lightly charred, 1 to 2 minutes. Transfer the lemon slices to the plate.

To prepare the rice, turn down the heat to medium-low and add the butter. When the butter has melted, add the wine and stir to scrape up any browned bits from the pan bottom. Add the shallot, garlic, and ½ tsp salt and cook, stirring occasionally, until the shallot is softened, about 2 minutes. Stir in the rice and cook, stirring, until fragrant and lightly toasted, about 1 minute.

To finish the dish, add the broth and lemon juice to the skillet and increase the heat to medium. Bring the mixture to a boil. Top with the browned chicken thighs, skinned-side up, in a single layer and arrange two lemon slices on top of each thigh. Cover the skillet with aluminum foil and then with a lid and turn down the heat to low. Simmer, without uncovering the skillet, for 20 minutes. Remove from the heat and let sit, covered, for 5 minutes. The rice will have absorbed the liquid and be tender and the chicken will be cooked through.

To serve, uncover the skillet and garnish with the olives and parsley.

Nutrition Values (per serving): Energy (kJ) ~2008 kJ, Calories ~480 kcal, Fat ~18 g, Saturated Fat ~6 g, Carbohydrate ~42 g, Sugar ~2 g, Dietary Fiber ~1 g, Protein ~34 g, Cholesterol ~115 mg, Sodium ~780 mg

New England Baked Fish

One of Culinary Team member Jay Chan's favorite comfort foods, this dish evokes Cape Cod summers, coastal breezes, and long, carefree afternoons. Growing up eating primarily Chinese and Vietnamese cuisine, Jay viewed this New England classic as instantly iconic. He featured it at his restaurant in Brooklyn as a way to relive those childhood summers, adding a mayonnaise-based topping for flavor, moisture, and structural stability during service. If you have a go-to tartar sauce, serve it alongside the fish for extra richness.

MAKES 4 SERVINGS

1 sleeve Ritz crackers (about 3½ oz/100 g)

4 Tbsp (55 g) unsalted butter, melted

2 Tbsp chopped fresh flat-leaf parsley

2 Tbsp sliced fresh chives

Kosher salt and freshly ground pepper

½ cup (120 g) mayonnaise

1 large egg yolk

1 garlic clove, minced

½ tsp chopped fresh thyme leaves

1 lemon

4 skinless cod or haddock fillets (6 to 8 oz/170 to 225 g each), pin bones removed

2 Tbsp dry white wine, such as Sancerre (optional)

Preheat the oven to 425°F (220°C).

To make the cracker topping, in a medium bowl, crush the crackers with your hands until mostly fine (some coarser bits are OK). Add the melted butter and 1 Tbsp each of the parsley and chives, then season with pepper. Stir until the cracker crumbs are evenly moistened and all the ingredients are well mixed.

To make the mayonnaise topping, in a small bowl, stir together the mayonnaise, egg yolk, garlic, and thyme. Finely grate the zest from half of the lemon into the bowl. Stir to combine. Cut the lemon into quarters and set aside for serving.

To prep the fish, pat it dry with paper towels and season all over with salt and pepper. Arrange the fish, skinned-side down, in a single layer in a large ovenproof skillet. Spread the mayonnaise topping evenly over fish fillets, dividing it evenly. Mound one-fourth of the cracker topping on top of each fillet, gently pressing it into the mayonnaise topping to adhere. If using the wine, pour it into the pan around the fish, avoiding the topping.

Bake the fish until it is just cooked through (barely opaque and still moist) and flakes easily with a fork, 10 to 15 minutes, depending on the thickness of the fillets.

To serve, transfer the fillets to four warmed plates. Garnish with the remaining 1 Tbsp each parsley and chives and serve the lemon quarters alongside.

Nutrition Values (per serving): Energy (kJ) ~2008 kJ, Calories ~480 kcal, Fat ~28 g, Saturated Fat ~8 g, Carbohydrate ~14 g, Sugar ~1 g, Dietary Fiber ~0 g, Protein ~38 g, Cholesterol ~115 mg, Sodium ~780 mg

Broccoli Cheddar Orzo Skillet

Cheesy, creamy, and packed with tender broccoli, this skillet meal is comfort in a pan. Nutty orzo pasta soaks up a rich blend of sharp Cheddar and savory broth, while onion, garlic, and a hint of mustard powder add a punch of flavor. If you use a whole head of broccoli, don't toss the stem. Cut off the woody base and peel the thick skin, then chop the stem into ½-inch (12-mm) pieces and cook them with the onion. This dish is best eaten when it is first made, but if you have leftovers, reheat over low heat, loosening the mixture with broth or milk as needed.

MAKES 4 SERVINGS

2 Tbsp olive oil

½ yellow onion, finely chopped

Kosher salt and freshly ground pepper

1 large broccoli crown (about 8 oz/225 g), chopped into small pieces

1 cup (6 oz/170 g) orzo

½ tsp granulated garlic

½ tsp yellow mustard powder

1¾ cups (415 ml) vegetable or chicken broth

½ cup (120 ml) whole milk, plus more if needed to thin

1 cup (120 g) shredded sharp Cheddar cheese

2 Tbsp unsalted butter

To cook the broccoli, in a deep, heavy 10-inch (25-cm) skillet over medium heat, warm the oil. Add the onion and a pinch of salt and cook, stirring occasionally, until the onion is tender and starts to brown, about 5 minutes. Add the broccoli, ½ tsp salt, and a few grinds of pepper and stir to combine. Cook, stirring, just until the florets are bright green, about 2 minutes.

To cook the orzo, add the orzo, garlic, and mustard powder to the skillet and cook, stirring constantly, until the orzo is lightly toasted, about 1 minute. Pour in the broth and stir to mix, scraping up any browned bits from the pan bottom. Bring the mixture to a boil, then turn down the heat to medium-low. Simmer gently, stirring often and scraping the bottom of the skillet occasionally, until the orzo is just shy of al dente and most of the liquid is absorbed, about 4 minutes.

To finish the dish, add the milk, stir to combine, and bring to a simmer. Slowly add the cheese, a handful at a time, stirring after each addition until melted. Stir in the butter until it melts and the mixture becomes saucy. If the mixture is too thick, loosen it with a little milk.

To serve, remove from the heat and let sit for a few minutes to allow the sauce to thicken, then spoon into four bowls.

Nutrition Values (per serving): Energy (kJ) ~1799 kJ, Calories ~430 kcal, Fat ~20 g, Saturated Fat ~9 g, Carbohydrate ~46 g, Sugar ~4 g, Dietary Fiber ~3 g, Protein ~14 g, Cholesterol ~40 mg, Sodium ~620 mg

Balsamic Steak, Mushroom & Potato Skillet

Here, marinated sirloin steak tips, earthy cremini mushrooms, and buttery Yukon Gold potatoes are cooked separately in the same skillet. Then, just before serving, they are tossed and stirred together in that same pan and drizzled with a sticky, tangy balsamic glaze that's bursting with garlicky, sweet, and savory notes, creating a one-skillet meal that's bold, rich, and irresistible.

MAKES 4 SERVINGS

¼ cup (60 ml) soy sauce or tamari

¼ cup (60 ml) balsamic vinegar

1 Tbsp packed light brown sugar

1 Tbsp whole-grain mustard

2 garlic cloves, minced

Kosher salt and freshly ground pepper

1½ lb (680 g) sirloin steak, cut into 1-inch (2.5-cm) pieces

1 lb (450 g) small Yukon Gold or other yellow potatoes, unpeeled, cut into 1-inch (2.5-cm) chunks

Olive oil, for drizzling

8 oz (225 g) small cremini mushrooms, stem ends trimmed, then halved or quartered if large

1 Tbsp chopped fresh rosemary

2 Tbsp unsalted butter

Preheat the oven to 425°F (220°C).

To marinate the steak, in a bowl, whisk together the soy sauce, vinegar, sugar, mustard, garlic, ¼ tsp salt, and ½ tsp pepper. Add the steak and stir to coat evenly. Set aside for 30 minutes.

To roast the potatoes, in a large ovenproof skillet, toss the potatoes with a drizzle of oil, coating evenly, then season with salt and pepper. Transfer to the oven and roast, stirring occasionally, until the potatoes are tender, about 25 minutes. Transfer the potatoes to a bowl.

To make the glaze, drain off the marinade from the steak into a small saucepan and place the pan over medium heat. Bring to a boil, stirring, until the marinade becomes syrupy, about 4 minutes. Set aside.

To cook the steak, place the skillet over high heat and drizzle with a little oil. Pat the steak pieces dry with paper towels. When the oil is shimmering, add half of the steak pieces in a single layer and cook, stirring once or twice, until browned and medium-rare, about 2 minutes. Transfer the steak to a plate and repeat with the remaining steak, adding more oil to the pan if needed.

To cook the mushrooms, turn down the heat to medium, add a drizzle of oil to the skillet, and then add the mushrooms and rosemary. Cook, stirring occasionally, until the mushrooms are tender, about 5 minutes.

To finish, add the butter to the skillet and stir until melted. Then add the cooked potatoes and the steak and its juices to the skillet and toss and stir all the ingredients, mixing well. Drizzle with as much of the syrupy marinade as you like and cook, stirring, until heated through. Serve at once.

Nutrition Values (per serving): Energy (kJ) 2300kJ, Calories 550 kcal, Fat 28 g, Saturated Fat 9 g, Carbohydrate 32 g, Sugar 7 g, Dietary Fiber 4 g, Protein 38 g, Cholesterol 125 mg, Sodium 980 mg

4 Bountiful Bowls

“We need recipes that deliver on flavor without demanding hours in the kitchen.”

–Sara Heilman, HelloFresh Test Kitchen

There's something wonderfully satisfying about a meal served in a single bowl. It's the ultimate culinary hug and a delicious landscape where every ingredient plays its part, piled high, mixed together, or layered for the perfect bite. Welcome to the chapter dedicated to the simple, comforting, and incredibly versatile magic of a complete meal in a bowl.

In our bustling lives, we need recipes that deliver on flavor without demanding hours in the kitchen. That's the heart of this collection. We've taken inspiration from across the globe, transforming classic dishes and creating new family favorites that are both easy to prepare and guaranteed to leave everyone feeling nourished and happy. From weeknight dinners to weekend lunches, these bowls are designed to make home cooking joyful and accessible.

You'll find flavor-packed dinners like Korean Beef Bibimbap with Zucchini, Mushrooms & Carrots, a customizable masterpiece of layered meat, vegetables, and rice, and the quick-to-assemble HelloFresh favorite, Firecracker Meatballs & Sesame Rice Bowl. We believe that bowls can offer something for everyone. Craving comfort? Dig into the creamy, rich Cheddar Veggie Soup or the classic, soul-soothing Matzo Ball Soup. For a lighter, plant-forward option, look to the Maple Carrot Power Bowl with Couscous or the protein-rich Coconut Rice Bowl with Tofu & Peanut Sauce, which offers a delicious journey of textures and tastes.

What makes a great bowl? It's often the deliberate combination of a wholesome base (rice, quinoa, couscous, or pasta), a hearty protein, fresh vegetables, and, critically, a killer sauce or dressing that ties everything together. Think of the tangy, citrus-forward dressing on the Ginger-Lemon Salmon Quinoa Bowl with Roasted Asparagus or the creamy nut-based sauce drizzled over the Coconut Rice Bowl with Tofu & Peanut Sauce. These are the elements that elevate a simple assembly of ingredients into a truly bountiful meal.

So grab a big spoon and your favorite bowl! Whether you're looking for a new family tradition or a quick, comforting meal after a long day, the recipes in this chapter prove that the simplest vessel can hold the most extraordinary flavors. Let's get cooking!

Korean Beef Bibimbap Rice Bowl with Zucchini, Mushrooms & Carrots

This dish takes its name from the Korean word for "mixing rice," and that's exactly how it's meant to be enjoyed: Rice is layered with ground beef, carrots, zucchini, and mushrooms, topped with a savory sauce, and then "mixed" so every bite is a harmonious blend of flavors and textures. Vibrant and flavorful, bibimbap is fun to eat and easy to customize with your own vegetable choices, like swapping shiitake mushrooms for the button mushrooms or spinach instead of zucchini. For extra protein, top each bowl with an egg fried sunny-side up.

MAKES 4 SERVINGS

2½ cups (590 ml) water

1½ cups (300 g) jasmine rice

Kosher salt and freshly ground pepper

4 scallions, white and green parts, thinly sliced and parts kept separate

3 Tbsp white wine vinegar

2 Tbsp toasted sesame oil

2 Tbsp sugar

4 tsp sriracha sauce

6 Tbsp (90 ml) soy sauce

Vegetable oil, for cooking

2 medium carrots, peeled and shaved lengthwise into ribbons with a vegetable peeler

2 medium zucchini, halved lengthwise and cut crosswise into thin half-moons

8 oz (225 g) button mushrooms, stem ends trimmed and thinly sliced

4 garlic cloves, minced

1 Tbsp peeled and minced fresh ginger

1¼ lb (570 g) ground beef

To make the rice, in a saucepan over medium-high heat, bring the water to a boil. Add the rice and a generous pinch of salt. Cover, turn down the heat to low, and cook until the water is absorbed and the rice is tender, 15 to 20 minutes. Remove from the heat and set aside, covered, to keep warm.

To marinate the scallions, in a small bowl, combine the scallion whites, vinegar, and a pinch of salt and toss to mix. Set aside to marinate.

To make the sauce, in another small bowl, stir together the sesame oil, sugar, 2 tsp of the sriracha, and 3 Tbsp of the soy sauce until the sugar dissolves.

To cook the vegetables, in a large skillet (preferably nonstick) over medium-high heat, warm a drizzle of vegetable oil. When the oil is shimmering, add the carrot ribbons and season with salt and pepper. Cook, tossing occasionally, until tender but still crisp, 3 to 4 minutes. Transfer to a large plate.

With the skillet still over medium-high heat, warm another drizzle of vegetable oil. Add the zucchini and season with salt and pepper. Cook, stirring occasionally, until tender-crisp, 3 to 4 minutes. Transfer to the plate with the carrots, keeping them separate.

continued . . .

Korean Beef Bibimbap Rice Bowl with Zucchini, Mushrooms & Carrots

continued from page 118 . . .

With the skillet still over medium-high heat, warm another drizzle of vegetable oil. Add the mushrooms and cook, stirring occasionally, until tender, 3 to 5 minutes. Season with salt and pepper. Transfer to the plate with the carrots and zucchini, keeping them separate.

To cook the beef, with the skillet still over medium-high heat, warm another drizzle of oil. Add the garlic and ginger and cook, stirring, until fragrant, about 30 seconds. Add the beef and cook, stirring and breaking up the meat with a wooden spoon as it cooks, until it is no longer pink, about 4 minutes. Increase the heat to high and continue cooking, stirring occasionally, until browned and crisp, about 3 minutes. Pour in the remaining 3 Tbsp soy sauce and cook, stirring, until most of the liquid has evaporated, 1 to 2 minutes. Season with salt and pepper.

To assemble and serve, divide the rice evenly among four bowls. Arrange the beef, zucchini, carrot, mushrooms, and scallion whites on top. Drizzle with the reserved sauce and the remaining 2 tsp sriracha, dividing them evenly. Sprinkle with the scallion greens and serve.

Nutrition Values (per serving): Energy (kJ) 3389 kJ, Calories 810 kcal, Fat 36 g, Saturated Fat 10 g, Carbohydrate 90 g, Sugar 18 g, Dietary Fiber 5 g, Protein 35 g, Cholesterol 90 mg, Sodium 1020 mg

Herbed Quinoa Bowl

Herb-flecked, protein-packed quinoa is layered with tender greens in this hearty and nutritious bowl, which is then topped with creamy avocado slices, jammy boiled eggs, crisp cucumber, and crunchy pepitas for add richness and texture. A zesty Dijon vinaigrette brings everything together.

MAKES 4 SERVINGS

DIJON VINAIGRETTE

2 Tbsp extra virgin olive oil

2 Tbsp vegetable oil

3 Tbsp white wine vinegar

1 Tbsp Dijon mustard

½ tsp agave nectar or honey

Kosher salt

QUINOA SALAD

1 cup (180 g) quinoa

2 cups (475 ml) water

Kosher salt and freshly ground pepper

4 large eggs

5 oz (140 g) roughly chopped baby kale, arugula, and/or mixed greens (about 6 cups)

2 scallions, white and green parts, finely chopped

4 Tbsp (10 g) chopped fresh cilantro leaves

4 Tbsp (10 g) chopped fresh mint leaves

2 ripe avocados, halved, pitted, peeled, and thinly sliced

½ English or Kirby cucumber, thinly sliced

½ cup (70 g) toasted pepitas (optional)

To make the vinaigrette, in a jar, combine the ingredients, cap tightly, and shake vigorously until well blended. Season with salt, then taste and adjust the seasoning with more agave nectar and salt if needed.

To cook the quinoa, in a small saucepan, combine the quinoa, water, and ½ tsp salt and bring to a boil over high heat, stirring once or twice. Turn down the heat to low, cover, and cook until tender and the water has been completely absorbed, about 15 minutes. Uncover and fluff with a fork, then transfer to medium bowl. Drizzle with 2 Tbsp of the vinaigrette and toss until evenly coated. Let cool completely.

To boil the eggs, fill a saucepan with enough water to cover the eggs completely and bring to a boil over medium-high heat. Fill a bowl with ice and water for an ice bath and set it near the stove. Using a slotted spoon, lower the eggs into the boiling water and cook for 7 to 8 minutes for eggs with set whites and jammy yolks. If you prefer a firmer yolk, cook for about 12 minutes. When the eggs are ready, transfer them to the ice bath to stop the cooking. Let sit until the eggs are cool enough to handle, then peel off the shells. Set aside.

To assemble and serve, add the kale to a bowl, drizzle with a little vinaigrette, and toss to coat. Divide the kale evenly among four shallow bowls. Add half of the scallions and 1 Tbsp each of the cilantro and mint to the quinoa and toss to mix. Taste and adjust the seasoning with salt and pepper if needed. Divide the mixture among the bowls, spooning the quinoa over the kale.

Top each serving with a sliced avocado half, fanning out the slices; one-fourth of the cucumber slices; and an egg, cut in half. Sprinkle the avocado and egg with salt and pepper. Drizzle some vinaigrette over each bowl, then garnish with the remaining cilantro, mint, and scallions, dividing them evenly. Garnish with the pepitas, if using, and serve.

Nutrition Values (per serving): Energy (kJ) ~2008 kJ, Calories ~480 kcal, Fat ~32 g, Saturated Fat ~4 g, Carbohydrate ~36 g, Sugar ~2 g, Dietary Fiber ~8 g, Protein ~14 g, Cholesterol 0 mg (plant-based), Sodium ~450 mg

Grilled Vegetable Pasta Salad

This Italian pasta salad shines with the flavors of summer. Sweet corn, zucchini, and red bell peppers are grilled until lightly charred, bringing smoky sweetness, while juicy cherry tomatoes, marinated artichokes, and briny Kalamata olives add layers of brightness. They are all tossed with your choice of short pasta, a zesty dressing, crumbled feta, and fresh herbs to create a dish that's ideal for backyard dinners, seaside picnics, or summer afternoons.

MAKES 6 SERVINGS

12 oz (340 g) small shaped pasta, such as fusilli, cavatelli, or penne

4 Tbsp (60 ml) extra virgin olive oil, plus more for brushing

1 medium zucchini, cut lengthwise into planks ½ inch (12 mm) thick

2 ears corn, husks and silk removed

1 small red bell pepper

Kosher salt and freshly ground black pepper

2 cups (340 g) halved cherry tomatoes (about 12 oz)

1 (7-oz/200-g) jar marinated artichoke hearts, drained and chopped

¼ cup (45 g) chopped pitted Kalamata olives

¼ cup (60 ml) fresh lime juice

¾ cup (85 g) crumbled feta cheese

¼ cup (10 g) chopped fresh cilantro or flat-leaf parsley

To cook the pasta, bring a large pot of salted water to a boil over high heat. Add the pasta, bring the water back to a boil, and cook, stirring occasionally, until al dente, according to package directions. Drain and rinse well under cold running water, then drain well again and transfer to a large serving bowl. Drizzle with 2 Tbsp of the oil.

Prepare a charcoal or gas grill for direct cooking over medium-high heat (400° to 450°F/200° to 230°C). When the grill is ready, brush the grill grates clean.

To prep the vegetables, arrange the zucchini planks, ears of corn, and bell pepper in a single layer on a large sheet pan. Brush each lightly with oil, then season with salt.

To grill the vegetables, place them in a single layer on the grill grates directly over the fire, close the lid, and grill, turning occasionally, until nicely etched with grill marks and tender-crisp, about 4 minutes for the zucchini, 9 minutes for the corn, and 10 minutes for the pepper. As the vegetables are ready, transfer them to a cutting board, putting the pepper into a small bowl and covering it with a plate.

When the vegetables are cool enough to handle, cut the corn kernels from the cobs and dice the zucchini. Peel and rub off the blackened skin from the bell pepper, then cut out and discard the stem, core, and seeds. Dice the pepper.

To assemble the salad, add the grilled vegetables to the pasta along with the tomatoes, artichokes, and olives. Drizzle with the remaining 2 Tbsp olive oil and the lime juice and toss to mix evenly. Add the feta and cilantro and season with salt and pepper. Toss again, then serve.

Nutrition Values (per serving): Energy (kJ) ~1506 kJ, Calories ~360 kcal, Fat ~18 g, Saturated Fat ~4 g, Carbohydrate ~40 g, Sugar ~4 g, Dietary Fiber ~4 g, Protein ~9 g, Cholesterol 0 mg, Sodium ~520 mg

Cheddar Veggie Soup

Rich, creamy, and packed with fresh vegetables, this soup is especially welcome on a cold-weather evening. Packed with Yukon Gold potatoes, broccoli, cauliflower, carrots, leek, and celery that are brightened with white wine, this surprisingly light Cheddar soup feels luxurious because of its velvety texture. Have fun swapping out the vegetables included here for whatever you have on hand in your refrigerator crisper drawer.

MAKES 4 TO 6 SERVINGS

8 oz (225 g) small Yukon Gold or other yellow potatoes, peeled, quartered lengthwise and cut crosswise into slices ¼ inch (6 mm) thick

Kosher salt and freshly ground pepper

6 Tbsp (85 g) unsalted butter

½ red onion, finely chopped

1 cup (115 g) finely chopped broccoli (about 4 oz)

1 cup (140 g) finely chopped cauliflower (about 5 oz)

2 small carrots, finely diced

1 leek, white and pale green parts, chopped

1 large celery stalk, finely diced

⅓ cup (45 g) all-purpose flour

2 Tbsp dry white wine

2 cups (475 ml) vegetable or chicken broth

2 cups (240 g) Cheddar cheese, shredded

¾ cup (175 ml) whole milk, plus more if needed

1 Tbsp Worcestershire sauce

Chopped fresh chives or flat-leaf parsley, for garnish

To cook the potatoes, put the potatoes into a small saucepan, add water to cover and 1½ tsp salt, and bring to a boil over medium-high heat. Cook, stirring occasionally, until the potatoes are tender, 5 to 6 minutes. Drain and set aside.

To cook the remaining vegetables, in a large, heavy pot over medium heat, melt 2 Tbsp of the butter. Add the onion and cook, stirring, for 2 minutes. Add the broccoli, cauliflower, carrots, leek, and celery and sprinkle generously with salt, then cook, stirring occasionally, until the vegetables are just tender, about 7 minutes. Transfer the vegetables to a medium bowl, add the reserved potatoes, and set aside.

To make the cheddar soup base, with the pot still over medium heat, add the remaining 4 Tbsp (55 g) butter. When the butter has melted, whisk in the flour until well mixed, then continue to cook, stirring, until the mixture turns golden brown, about 2 minutes. Slowly whisk in the wine and then the broth, whisking until the mixture is smooth. Bring to a gentle boil, then turn down the heat to medium-low and cook, stirring, until the mixture thickens slightly, about 3 minutes. Add the cheese by the handful, stirring with the whisk after each addition, until the cheese has melted and the mixture is well mixed and smooth. Stir in the milk, Worcestershire sauce, ½ tsp salt, and a generous amount of pepper.

To assemble and serve, return the vegetables to the pot and stir to combine. Bring to a simmer over medium heat, stirring, until the vegetables are heated through and the soup is piping hot. You can leave the soup chunky, or use an immersion blender to puree it to your liking. Adjust the thickness with more milk if needed, then ladle into bowls, garnish with chives, and serve.

Nutrition Values (per serving for 6 servings): Energy (kJ) ~2050 kJ, Calories ~490 kcal, Fat ~32 g, Saturated Fat ~19 g, Carbohydrate ~32 g, Sugar ~8 g, Dietary Fiber ~5 g, Protein ~15 g, Cholesterol ~95 mg, Sodium ~720 mg

Matzo Ball Soup

A centerpiece of every Rosh Hashanah and Passover, this comforting matzo ball soup is a cherished legacy passed down to Isabelle Zucker's aunt, Ruth Raskin, from her mother, Belle Zucker Gruber. Every year, Isabelle, a culinary product strategist at HelloFresh, joins over thirty extended family members at Ruth's table to share in this tradition. With its rich, slow-simmered chicken broth and light-as-air matzo balls, this soup warms both body and spirit. Garnish the finished soup with chopped scallions or ribbons of carrot peeled with a vegetable peeler.

MAKES 6 SERVINGS

CHICKEN BROTH

6 lb (2.7 kg) chicken parts, such as wings, necks, backs, and legs

4 qt (3.8 L) water

2 large yellow onions, peeled and quartered

2 large carrots, cut into thirds

2 large celery stalks with leaves, cut into thirds

1 small parsnip, halved

8 fresh flat-leaf parsley sprigs

3 fresh dill sprigs

Kosher salt and freshly ground pepper

2 chicken bouillon cubes (optional)

MATZO BALLS

3 large eggs, separated

¼ cup (60 ml) chicken broth

¼ cup (60 ml) schmaltz (rendered chicken fat) or vegetable oil, at room temperature

1 tsp plus 2 Tbsp kosher salt

¼ tsp freshly ground black pepper

¾ cup (90 g) fine matzo meal

4 qt (3.8 L) water

To make the broth, in a large pot, combine the chicken and water and bring to a boil over medium-high heat. Turn down the heat to medium-low to maintain a steady simmer, then, using a large metal spoon, skim off and discard any foam and other impurities that rise to the surface.

Add the onions, carrots, celery, parsnip, parsley, dill, 2 Tbsp salt, and a few grinds of pepper. Bring the broth back to a boil, then turn down the heat to low to maintain a gentle simmer and simmer, uncovered and skimming the surface occasionally to remove foam and other impurities, for at least 6 hours or preferably overnight. (If simmering overnight, add an additional 4 cups/950 ml water.)

Taste and season with more salt and pepper if needed. If the broth is not rich enough, boil down further and/or add the chicken bouillon cubes. Remove from the heat and let cool slightly. Using a large slotted spoon or tongs, lift out and discard the large pieces of vegetables and chicken, then strain the broth through a fine-mesh sieve into a large bowl. You should have about 2½ qt (2.4 L) broth. The broth can be used right away, or let it cool to room temperature, transfer it to one or more airtight containers, and store in the refrigerator for up to 5 days or in the freezer for up to 3 months.

To make the matzo balls, in a large bowl, stir together the egg yolks, broth, schmaltz, 1 tsp of the salt, and ¼ tsp pepper. Cover and refrigerate for 30 minutes or up to 2 hours. Stir in the matzo meal, mixing well. Re-cover the bowl and return it to the refrigerator.

In a stand mixer fitted with the whisk attachment, or in a medium bowl with a handheld mixer, beat the egg whites on medium-high speed until they hold stiff peaks. Using two butter knives or a pastry cutter, cut the matzo mixture until it is crumbly. Using a rubber spatula, gently fold the egg whites into the matzo mixture just until blended, being careful not to overmix. It is OK if a few white streaks remain. Cover and refrigerate for 1 hour.

To cook the matzo balls, add the water and the remaining 2 Tbsp salt to a large pot and bring to a boil over medium-high heat. Meanwhile, remove the matzo mixture from the refrigerator. Have ready a sheet pan.

To shape each matzo ball, using wet hands, scoop up about 2 Tbsp of the mixture, roll into a golf ball–size ball, and set on the sheet pan. Repeat until all the mixture is used up, adding the balls to the sheet pan as they are shaped. The dough will expand, so don't be tempted to make the balls larger. You should have about 18 matzo balls.

Gently add the matzo balls to the boiling water, then cover the pot. When the water returns to a gentle boil, turn down the heat to medium-low and cook until the matzo balls have doubled in size, are floating on the surface, and are cooked through, about 45 minutes. To test for doneness, scoop out a ball and cut it in half. It should be a pale uniform color all the way through.

Just before the matzo balls are ready, reheat the broth in a medium saucepan over medium-high heat until steaming.

To serve, using a slotted spoon, divide the matzo balls evenly among six shallow bowls. Ladle the hot broth over the top and serve.

Nutrition Values (per serving): Energy (kJ) ~1340 kJ, Calories ~320 kcal, Fat ~14 g, Saturated Fat ~4 g, Carbohydrate ~24 g, Sugar ~3 g, Dietary Fiber ~2 g, Protein ~22 g, Cholesterol ~135 mg, Sodium ~1,200 mg

Maple Carrot Power Bowl with Couscous

Maple syrup is the secret to tonight's harissa-roasted carrots, giving them a light sweet glaze. Served bowl-style, they are joined by golden turmeric-toasted couscous, garlicky kale, and creamy hummus. Dried cranberries and crunchy walnuts add bursts of texture and flavor.

MAKES 4 SERVINGS

8 oz (225 g) curly kale, stemmed and chopped and patted dry

Olive oil, for drizzling

2 tsp garlic powder

Kosher salt and freshly ground pepper

1 cup (225 g) pearl couscous

½ tsp ground turmeric

2 tsp vegetable broth concentrate

2½ cups (590 ml) plus 2 Tbsp water

1½ lb (680 g) carrots, peeled and cut into slices ¼ inch (66 mm) thick on the diagonal

½ tsp harissa powder

2 Tbsp maple syrup

1 cup (240 g) hummus

Juice of ½ lemon, plus 4 lemon wedges, for serving

6 Tbsp (55 g) dried cranberries

¼ cup (30 g) chopped toasted walnuts

To make the crispy kale, position oven racks in the middle and upper third of the oven and preheat the oven to 350°F (175°C). Line two half sheet pans with aluminum foil. Divide the kale between the prepared sheet pans, drizzle with oil, and sprinkle each batch with half of the garlic powder. Season with salt and pepper and toss until evenly coated. Spread the kale in an even layer. Place one pan on the upper rack and one on the middle rack and roast the kale, switching the pans between the racks halfway through cooking, until browned and crisp, 13 to 15 minutes. Remove from the oven and set aside.

To cook the couscous, in a saucepan over medium-high heat, warm a drizzle of oil. Add the couscous and ½ tsp of the turmeric and cook, stirring occasionally, until toasted, 1 to 2 minutes. Add the broth concentrate, 2¼ cups (530 ml) of the water, and a big pinch of salt and stir to combine. Bring to a boil, cover, turn down the heat to low, and cook until the couscous is tender, 8 to 12 minutes. Drain off any liquid.

To make the carrots, in a large skillet over medium-high heat, warm a generous drizzle of oil. Add the carrots and harissa powder, then season with salt and pepper. Cook, stirring occasionally, until just softened, 5 to 8 minutes. Add the maple syrup and ¼ cup (60 ml) of the water and cook, stirring occasionally, until the carrots are lightly browned and tender, 3 to 5 minutes. Remove from the heat.

To make the hummus, in a bowl, combine the hummus, lemon juice, 2 Tbsp oil, and the remaining 2 Tbsp water and stir until well mixed.

To assemble, fluff the couscous with a fork and stir in a drizzle of oil. Season with salt and pepper. Divide the couscous among four bowls. Top each bowl with the kale and carrots, dividing them evenly. Sprinkle the bowls with the cranberries and walnuts, then drizzle the hummus on top, dividing it evenly. Serve at once, with a lemon wedge on each bowl.

Nutrition Values (per serving): Calories 780 kcal, Fat 39 g, Saturated Fat 5 g, Carbohydrate 96 g, Sugar 30 g, Dietary Fiber 13 g, Protein 16 g, Sodium 580 mg

Firecracker Meatballs & Sesame Rice Bowl

This recipe reimagines everything you thought you knew about meatballs. The real star is the firecracker sauce, a creamy, sweet-spicy glaze that goes together in a flash. After roasting, the meatballs are tossed in the sauce, served over sesame rice, and accompanied with crispy roasted green beans, with the rice soaking up every last drop of the irresistible sauce.

MAKES 4 SERVINGS

FIRECRACKER SAUCE

¼ cup (60 g) sour cream
¼ cup (60 g) mayonnaise
4 tsp honey
4 tsp soy sauce
2 tsp sriracha sauce

RICE

Vegetable oil, for cooking
1 Tbsp sesame seeds
1 cup (200 g) jasmine rice
1½ cups (360 ml) water
Kosher salt and freshly ground pepper

MEATBALLS

4 scallions
1¼ lb (570 g) ground beef
½ cup (30 g) panko breadcrumbs
1-inch (2.5-cm) piece fresh ginger, peeled and minced
2 Tbsp plus 2 tsp soy sauce
Kosher salt and freshly ground pepper
12 oz (340 g) green beans, trimmed
Vegetable oil, for drizzling
1 Tbsp sesame seeds
Gochugaru (Korean chile flakes), for garnish

Position one oven rack in the middle and one in the upper third of the oven and preheat the oven to 425°F (220°C).

To make the firecracker sauce, in a bowl, stir together the sour cream, mayonnaise, honey, soy sauce, and sriracha, mixing well. Set aside.

To make the rice, in a saucepan over medium-high heat, warm a drizzle of oil. Add the sesame seeds and cook, stirring, until golden brown, 1 to 2 minutes. Add the rice, water, and a big pinch of salt and bring to a boil. Cover, turn down the heat to low, and cook until the liquid is absorbed and the rice is tender, about 20 minutes. Remove from the heat and keep covered until ready to serve.

Make the meatballs and green beans while the rice cooks. Lightly oil two large sheet pans. Thinly slice the green parts and mince the white parts of the scallions and keep the parts separate. In a large bowl, mix together the beef, panko, ginger, scallion whites, soy sauce, 1 tsp salt, and several grinds of pepper. Form into twenty to twenty-four 1½-inch (4-cm) balls, spacing them apart on one of the prepared sheet pans.

On the second sheet pan, toss the green beans with a drizzle of oil, and season with salt and pepper. Spread the beans in a single layer. Place the pan with the green beans on the top rack of the oven and the pan with the meatballs on the middle rack. Roast until the meatballs are cooked through and the green beans are tender, 14 to 16 minutes.

To assemble and serve, season the rice with salt and pepper and divide among four bowls. Add the meatballs to the firecracker sauce and toss to coat. Top the rice with the green beans and meatballs, dividing evenly and drizzling them with any sauce in the bowl. Garnish the with the scallion greens, sesame seeds, and chile flakes.

Nutrition Values (per serving): Energy (kJ) 3264 kJ, Calories 780 kcal, Fat 44 g, Saturated Fat 14 g, Carbohydrate 63 g, Sugar 13 g, Dietary Fiber 3 g, Protein 33 g, Cholesterol 125 mg, Sodium 1510 mg

Coconut Rice Bowl with Tofu & Peanut Sauce

This rice bowl uses black rice, also known as forbidden rice, which is a whole grain with a nutty flavor, chewy texture, and striking deep purple color. For this bowl, it's cooked in coconut milk for a subtly sweet base. Swap in white or brown rice if you like and cook according to package directions. Golden seared tofu, sautéed spinach, and a velvety peanut sauce top it all off.

MAKES 4 SERVINGS

COCONUT BLACK RICE

1 cup (180 g) black rice (forbidden rice), rinsed

1 (13.5-fl oz/405-ml) can coconut milk, well shaken

1 tsp kosher salt

PEANUT SAUCE

½ cup (130 g) unsweetened natural creamy peanut butter

2 Tbsp packed light brown sugar

1 Tbsp soy sauce

1 Tbsp rice vinegar

Juice of ½ lime

1 tsp peeled and grated fresh ginger

1 tsp sambal oelek

½ tsp toasted sesame oil

¼ cup (60 ml) water

SEARED TOFU AND SPINACH

1 (14- to 16-oz/400 to 450-g) block firm tofu, drained

1 Tbsp soy sauce or tamari

1½ Tbsp vegetable oil

5 to 8 oz (140 to 225 g) baby spinach

2 scallions, white and green parts, finely chopped

Kosher salt

To make the rice, add to a saucepan with the coconut milk and salt and bring to a boil over medium-high heat. Turn down the heat to low, cover, and cook for 40 minutes. Remove from the heat and set aside, covered, for 10 minutes. The rice is ready when the liquid is absorbed and the rice grains are tender but still slightly chewy.

To make the peanut sauce, in a blender, combine the ingredients and blend on medium speed until the mixture is smooth and thick, scraping down the sides a few times and adding more water if needed, until the sauce is smooth and thick but pourable. Set the sauce aside. (The sauce will keep in an airtight container in the refrigerator for up to 1 week.)

To make the tofu, cut the tofu into cubes. Transfer to a small bowl, drizzle with the soy sauce, and toss gently to coat evenly. Select a large, well-seasoned or nonstick skillet that will accommodate the tofu pieces in a single layer without crowding. Heat the pan over medium-high heat. When the pan is hot, add the tofu and cook until crisp and golden brown on the underside, about 3 minutes. Drizzle 1 Tbsp of the oil into the pan, then turn the tofu and cook until crisp and golden brown on the second side, about 3 minutes more. Transfer to a plate.

To cook the spinach, reduce the heat to medium and add the remaining ½ Tbsp oil. When the oil is shimmering, add the spinach and scallions and a pinch of salt and cook, stirring and tossing, just until the spinach is wilted, 1 to 2 minutes.

To assemble, fluff the rice with a fork, then divide among four bowls. Top with the tofu and spinach, dividing them evenly, then drizzle generously with the peanut sauce and serve, passing any remaining peanut sauce at the table.

Nutrition Values (per serving): Energy (kJ) ~2259 kJ, Calories ~540 kcal, Fat ~28 g, Saturated Fat ~10 g, Carbohydrate ~52 g, Sugar ~8 g, Dietary Fiber ~6 g, Protein ~20 g, Cholesterol ~0 mg, Sodium ~780 mg

Dumpling Udon Noodle Soup with Snow Peas & Scallions

This big bowl of dumpling noodle soup brings together plump gyoza, chewy udon noodles, and tender-crisp snow peas in a fragrant broth—and it couldn't be faster to throw together on a busy night. The broth is infused with warmth and spice from fresh ginger and garlic, umami notes from white miso, and bright flavor from scallions. If you cannot source fresh udon noodles, substitute 8 ounces (225 g) dried. Boil them in water in advance according to package directions, then add them to the soup at the last minute to warm through.

MAKES 4 SERVINGS

1 Tbsp vegetable oil

1 Tbsp peeled and finely grated fresh ginger

2 garlic cloves, minced

6 cups (1.4 L) chicken or vegetable broth

2 Tbsp white miso paste

Kosher salt

12 oz to 1 lb (340 to 450 g) frozen pork, chicken, or vegetable gyoza (12 to 16 dumplings)

1 lb (450 g) fresh udon noodles

4 oz (115 g) snow peas, trimmed and thickly sliced on the diagonal

2 scallions, white and green parts, thinly sliced

To make the broth, in a large saucepan over medium heat, combine the oil, ginger, and garlic and cook, stirring, until fragrant, about 1 minute. Pour in the broth and bring to a gentle boil. Adjust the heat to maintain a gentle simmer, cover, and simmer until the flavors come together, about 10 minutes. Whisk in the miso, then taste and season with salt if needed.

To cook the dumplings, noodles, and vegetables, add the dumplings to the gently simmering broth and bring the broth back to a gentle simmer. Do not let the broth come to a hard boil. When the dumplings float to the top and are heated through, after 3 to 4 minutes, add the noodles, snow peas, and scallions and cook, stirring gently, until the noodles are al dente and the dumplings are cooked, about 3 minutes longer, or according to package directions.

To serve, ladle the soup into four bowls, dividing the dumplings and noodles evenly. Serve at once.

Nutrition Values (per serving): Energy (kJ) ~1757 kJ, Calories ~420 kcal, Fat ~14 g, Saturated Fat ~3 g, Carbohydrate ~56 g, Sugar ~4 g, Dietary Fiber ~3 g, Protein ~18 g, Cholesterol ~35 mg, Sodium ~1,600 mg

Ginger-Lemon Salmon Quinoa Bowl with Roasted Asparagus

Fast, flavorful, and super easy, these salmon quinoa bowls are a weeknight winner. Tender salmon fillets are glazed with a bright, zesty mix of lemon, ginger, tamari, and a touch of brown sugar, then roasted alongside tender-crisp asparagus. Served over fluffy quinoa—or steamed white or brown rice for a swap—each bowl is a balanced mix of savory, tangy, and slightly sweet flavors.

MAKES 4 SERVINGS

1 cup (180 g) quinoa, rinsed and drained

2 cups (475 ml) water

Kosher salt and freshly ground pepper

4 skinless salmon fillets (about 6 oz/170 g each), pin bones removed

¼ cup (60 ml) reduced-sodium tamari or soy sauce

Finely grated zest and juice of 1 lemon

1 Tbsp packed light brown sugar

1 tsp packed peeled and finely grated fresh ginger

1 lb (450 g) medium asparagus, woody ends trimmed

Olive oil, for drizzling

Preheat the oven to 425°F (220°C).

To make the quinoa, in a small saucepan, combine the quinoa, water, and ½ tsp salt and bring to a boil over high heat, stirring once or twice. Turn down the heat to low, cover, and cook until tender and the water has been completely absorbed, about 15 minutes.

To make the salmon and asparagus, while the quinoa is cooking, lightly oil a baking dish just large enough to hold the salmon in a single layer without touching. Arrange the fillets in the prepared dish. In a small bowl, whisk together the tamari, lemon zest and juice, brown sugar, and ginger until the sugar dissolves. Pour evenly over the salmon.

Place the asparagus on a small sheet pan. Drizzle with oil and season generously with salt and pepper, then toss to coat evenly. Spread in a single layer.

Roast the salmon for 8 minutes, then add the sheet pan with the asparagus to the oven. Continue to roast until the salmon is cooked through to your liking (we like it still slightly pink in the center; timing depends on how thick the fillets are) and the asparagus is tender-crisp, about 8 minutes longer.

To assemble, uncover the quinoa, fluff with a fork, and divide evenly among four shallow bowls. Top each quinoa portion with a salmon fillet and one-fourth of the asparagus. Strain the sauce remaining in the baking dish through a fine-mesh sieve into a small heatproof pitcher or measuring cup and pour over the salmon, then serve.

Nutrition Values (per serving): Energy (kJ) ~2008 kJ, Calories ~480 kcal, Fat ~18 g, Saturated Fat ~3 g, Carbohydrate ~38 g, Sugar ~4 g, Dietary Fiber ~5 g, Protein ~34 g, Cholesterol ~75 mg, Sodium ~720 mg

Crispy Parmesan Chicken Couscous Bowl with Roasted Carrots

Consider plain chicken breasts a thing of the past. Here, the tender white meat is transformed with a crisp Parmesan-and-paprika breadcrumb coating that goes together with minimal fuss. The chicken roasts alongside a pan of sliced carrots, which are tossed with fresh lemon juice and zest when they emerge from the oven. Then both the chicken and the carrots are served atop herb butter–dressed couscous.

MAKES 4 SERVINGS

4 small boneless, skinless chicken breasts (about 5 oz/140 g each)

½ cup (30 g) panko breadcrumbs

½ cup (15 g) grated Parmesan cheese

2 tsp hot or sweet smoked paprika

Olive oil, for drizzling

Kosher salt and freshly ground pepper

4 Tbsp (60 g) sour cream

1½ lb (680 g) carrots, peeled, halved or quartered lengthwise, and cut crosswise into 2-inch (5-cm) pieces

1 cup (8 oz/225 g) pearl couscous

2¼ cups (530 ml) water

4 Tbsp (55 g) Garlic Herb Butter (page 47)

4 scallions, white and green parts, thinly sliced and parts kept separate

1 lemon

Position one oven rack in the middle and one in the upper third of the oven and preheat the oven to 425°F (220°C). Have ready two sheet pans.

To prep the chicken, lay a chicken breast on a cutting board. Using the flat side of a meat mallet (or the bottom of a small, heavy skillet), gently pound the chicken to an even thickness of about ¼ inch (6 mm). Repeat with the remaining chicken breasts.

In a small bowl, combine the breadcrumbs, Parmesan, paprika, a generous drizzle of oil, and a generous pinch each of salt and pepper and stir until well mixed. Pat the chicken dry with paper towels, then season all over with salt and pepper. Arrange in a single layer, not touching, on one of the sheet pans. Spread the top of each chicken breast with 1 Tbsp of the sour cream. Mound one-fourth of the breadcrumb mixture on each breast, then spread in an even layer and press firmly to adhere.

To prep the carrots, add the carrots to the second sheet pan, drizzle generously with oil, season with salt and pepper, and toss to coat evenly. Spread the carrots in an even layer on the pan.

To roast the chicken and carrots, place the chicken on the middle rack and the carrots on the upper rack. Roast until the chicken is cooked through and carrots are browned and tender, 15 to 20 minutes. If the carrots are ready before the chicken, remove them from the oven and continue roasting the chicken.

continued . . .

"It's during lively moments around the dinner table, that I'm aware of the beauty of being together."

–Kristin

Crispy Parmesan Chicken Couscous Bowl with Roasted Carrots

continued from page 136 . . .

Meanwhile, make the couscous. In a small saucepan over medium-high heat, warm a drizzle of oil. Add the couscous and cook, stirring occasionally, until fragrant and toasted, 1 to 2 minutes. Add the water and a big pinch of salt and stir until well mixed. Bring to a boil, cover, turn down the heat to low, and cook until the liquid is absorbed and the couscous is tender, 8 to 12 minutes. Drain off any excess liquid.

In a small saucepan over medium heat, melt the butter. Add the scallion whites and cook, stirring, until softened, about 1 minute. Add to the couscous and stir and toss until evenly distributed. Season with salt and pepper.

When the chicken has finished cooking, let it rest for 5 minutes, then cut each breast crosswise into thick slices. Finely grate the zest from the lemon, then cut the lemon into five wedges. Toss the carrots with the lemon zest and the juice of one lemon wedge.

To assemble and serve, divide the couscous evenly among four shallow bowls. Top each bowl with a sliced chicken breast and one-fourth of the roasted carrots. Garnish the chicken with the scallion greens and set a lemon wedge at the side of each bowl. Serve at once.

Nutrition Values (per serving): Energy (kJ) 2887 kJ, Calories 690 kcal, Fat 33 g, Saturated Fat 15 g, Carbohydrate 60 g, Sugar 12 g, Dietary Fiber 8 g, Protein 40 g, Cholesterol 160 mg, Sodium 520 mg

Lime-Cilantro Rice Bowl with Chili Chicken

You might want to make this bowl for the jalapeño ranch alone. It's that good! The bowl itself is a vibrant mix of chili-dusted chicken, rice infused with lime and cilantro, and colorful toppings: black beans, fire-roasted corn, pico de gallo, cherry tomatoes, and creamy avocado. Toss the whole works with the bold jalapeño ranch, taste, and you'll be putting this bowl on next week's menu.

MAKES 4 SERVINGS

LIME-CILANTRO RICE

¼ cup (10 g) chopped cilantro

3 Tbsp fresh lime juice

1 cup (240 ml) water

1 tsp kosher salt

1 cup (200 g) medium-grain rice

CHILI-DUSTED CHICKEN

1½ lb (680 g) boneless, skinless chicken breasts

2 Tbsp chili powder

Kosher salt and freshly ground pepper

Extra virgin olive oil, for drizzling

TOPPINGS

1 (15-oz/430-g) can black beans, drained and rinsed

⅓ cup (45 g) corn kernels

¼ tsp ground cumin

¼ cup (60 g) pico de gallo or salsa

1 cup (170 g) halved cherry tomatoes

1 large ripe avocado, halved, pitted, peeled, and sliced

Jalapeño ranch dressing (page 156), for serving

To make the rice, in a blender, combine the cilantro, lime juice, water, and salt and blend on high speed until smooth. Pour into a measuring jug, add water as needed to make 1½ cups (360 ml), and stir to mix. Add to a saucepan with the rice. Stir, cover, and place the pan over medium-high heat. When the mixture comes to a boil, turn down the heat to low, cover, and cook until the liquid is absorbed and the rice is tender, about 20 minutes. Set aside, covered, for 10 minutes.

To prep the chicken, lay a chicken breast on a cutting board. Using the flat side of a meat mallet, gently pound the chicken to an even thickness of about ¾ inch (2 cm). Transfer to a plate. Repeat with the remaining chicken. Season the breasts all over with the chili powder and with salt and pepper, then drizzle with oil on both sides.

To sear the chicken, heat a large, heavy skillet over medium heat. Add the chicken breasts and sear until nicely browned on the bottom, about 4 minutes. Turn, cover the skillet, and sear on the second side until browned and the chicken is cooked through but still juicy, about 4 minutes longer. Transfer to a cutting board and let rest for 5 minutes.

To make the beans for topping, while the chicken rests, in a small saucepan over medium heat, combine the beans, corn, and cumin, season with salt and pepper, and bring to a simmer, then simmer until warmed through. Remove from the heat and stir in the pico de gallo.

To assemble, divide the rice among four bowls. Cut the chicken crosswise into slices. Top with one-fourth of the chicken on one side of each bowl and the bean mixture on the other side of each bowl, dividing it evenly. Top each bowl with one-fourth each of the cherry tomatoes and avocado, then drizzle with ranch dressing and serve.

Nutrition Values (per serving): Energy (kJ) ~2594 kJ, Calories ~620 kcal, Fat ~22 g, Saturated Fat ~4 g, Carbohydrate ~58 g, Sugar ~6 g, Dietary Fiber ~9 g, Protein ~42 g, Cholesterol ~115 mg, Sodium ~950 mg

5 Sensational Salads

“The ingredients of the season will fill your basket with color.”

–Kristin

For years, salads carried an unfair reputation of being predictable and maybe even a little boring. But that's never been my experience. As someone who practically lives for weekend trips to the farmers' market, I've always seen salads as the most joyful expression of what's in season. There's nothing more inspiring than wandering past crates of sun-warmed tomatoes, crisp lettuces still smelling of the field, jewel-toned radishes, or herbs so fragrant you know you are near them before you even see them. That abundance of color and texture is where the best salads begin.

A sensational salad is a small act of delight. It's the sweet pop of berries you picked out that morning, the crunch of just-pulled carrots, the way a handful of fresh herbs can transform an ordinary bowl into something special. It's the textures and contrasts—creamy, crisp, juicy, tender—that make every bite an adventure. And it's the simple pleasure of knowing the ingredients you're using were grown with care and harvested at their peak.

This chapter is a celebration of that feeling—of the spark of creativity and connection that comes from cooking with the freshest ingredients you can get your hands on. These recipes are built for real life: weeknight friendly, generous, and absolutely bursting with color. Some are hearty enough to be dinner on their own, while others are bright sidekicks that elevate whatever else you're cooking.

Whether you're drawn to crunchy slaws, leafy greens, hearty grains, or unexpected flavor pairings, I hope these salads bring the joy of the farmers' market into your kitchen one colorful, delicious bowl at a time.

—Kristin

Kale Cobb Salad

A classic Cobb salad is all about crisp lettuce, bacon, eggs, avocado, and cheese. This version takes it up a notch with hearty dinosaur kale (also known as lacinato kale) in place of the iceberg. The kale adds earthy depth and a nice bite, while a bright lemon and balsamic dressing lifts the rich bacon, creamy avocado, and tangy blue cheese. Finished with cherry tomatoes, cucumber half-moons, and perfectly boiled jammy eggs, it's a nutrient-packed twist on a beloved favorite.

MAKES 4 SERVINGS

6 slices thick-cut bacon, chopped

4 large eggs

2 bunches dinosaur kale (about 1 lb/450 g)

Finely grated zest and juice of ½ lemon

2 Tbsp extra virgin olive oil, plus more for drizzling

2 Tbsp balsamic vinegar, plus more for drizzling

Kosher salt and freshly ground pepper

1 cup (170 g) halved cherry tomatoes

1 large ripe avocado, halved, pitted, peeled, and cubed

½ English cucumber, halved lengthwise and thinly sliced crosswise into half-moons

4 oz (115 g) blue or feta cheese, crumbled (about 1 cup)

To cook the bacon, in a small skillet over medium heat, fry the bacon, stirring occasionally, until crisp, about 5 minutes. Using a slotted spoon, transfer to paper towels to drain.

To boil the eggs, fill a saucepan with enough water to cover the eggs completely and bring to a boil over medium-high heat. Fill a medium bowl with ice and water for an ice bath and set it near the stove. Using a slotted spoon, lower the eggs into the boiling water and cook for 7 to 8 minutes for eggs with set whites and jammy yolks. If you prefer a firmer yolk, cook for about 12 minutes. When the eggs are ready, use the slotted spoon to transfer them to the ice bath to stop the cooking. Let sit until the eggs are cool enough to handle, then peel off the shells.

To prep the kale, while the eggs are cooling, strip the stems from the leaves and discard. Roughly chop the leaves and transfer to a large, wide bowl. Add the lemon zest and juice, oil, and vinegar and season with salt. Using your hands, massage the kale until it starts to look wilted, about 1 minute. Taste and adjust the seasoning with salt if needed.

To assemble and serve, divide the kale among four wide, shallow bowls. Dividing them evenly, arrange the bacon, tomatoes, avocado, cucumber, and cheese decoratively on top of the kale. Halve or quarter the eggs and add one to each bowl. Drizzle with a little more balsamic and oil, then season with salt and pepper. Serve at once.

Nutrition Values (per serving): Energy (kJ) ~2176 kJ, Calories ~520 kcal, Fat ~38 g, Saturated Fat ~11 g, Carbohydrate ~18 g, Sugar ~6 g, Dietary Fiber ~7 g, Protein ~20 g, Cholesterol ~230 mg, Sodium ~1,050 mg

Spinach Salad with Grilled Chicken, Crispy Chickpeas & Honey Mustard Dressing

Baby spinach, grilled chicken, and crispy chickpeas are dressed with a sweet-tangy dressing for this hearty main-course salad. For a vegetarian version, swap out the chicken for roasted sweet potatoes or butternut squash (page 54). Or to elevate both texture and color, add crisply cooked bacon or sliced heirloom tomatoes. No time to grill the chicken? Use shredded cooked chicken instead.

MAKES 4 SERVINGS

HONEY MUSTARD DRESSING

3 Tbsp extra virgin olive oil

2 Tbsp vegetable oil

2 Tbsp country Dijon mustard

1 Tbsp honey

1 Tbsp apple cider vinegar

Kosher salt and freshly ground pepper

CRISPY CHICKPEAS

1 (15-oz/430-g) can chickpeas, drained and rinsed

1 Tbsp extra virgin olive oil

Kosher salt and freshly ground pepper

SALAD

Grilled Chicken Breasts (page 38)

5 oz (140 g) baby spinach

1 small English cucumber, thinly sliced

¼ red onion, very thinly sliced

½ cup (60 g) crumbled feta cheese

Chopped fresh dill, chives, or parsley, or a mixture, for garnish

To make the dressing, in a jar, combine both oils, the mustard, honey, and vinegar, cap tightly, and shake vigorously until well blended. Season with salt and pepper.

To make the crispy chickpeas, spread the chickpeas on a large plate and pat dry with paper towels. In a medium skillet over medium heat, warm the oil. When the oil is shimmering, add the chickpeas and cook, stirring occasionally, until crisp and golden brown, about 4 minutes. Return the chickpeas to the plate and season with salt and pepper. Let cool.

To assemble the salad, slice the chicken thinly across the grain. In a large bowl, combine the spinach, chicken, chickpeas, cucumber, and red onion. Drizzle with half of the dressing and toss to coat. Garnish with the feta and herbs and serve, passing the remaining dressing at the table.

Nutrition Values (per serving): Energy (kJ) 2000 kJ, Calories 475 kcal, Fat 31 g, Saturated Fat 5 g, Carbohydrate 28 g, Sugar 8 g, Dietary Fiber 6 g, Protein 28 g, Cholesterol 65 mg, Sodium 620 mg

Lemongrass Pork & Rice Vermicelli Salad

This riff on Vietnamese barbecue pork bun bowls contains fragrant and subtly sweet lemongrass-marinated pork over delicate rice vermicelli and crisp cabbage salad. Fresh herbs, crunchy peanuts, and a bright, tangy Vietnamese sauce deliver layers of flavor and texture in every bite. Trade out the pork for chicken, or use romaine instead of cabbage for a different crunch.

MAKES 4 SERVINGS

LEMONGRASS PORK

2 large garlic cloves, chopped

1 shallot, chopped

1 lemongrass stalk, tender parts only, roughly chopped (3 Tbsp)

2 Tbsp packed light brown sugar

1 Tbsp fish sauce

1 Tbsp vegetable oil, plus more for cooking

1 Tbsp soy sauce or tamari

1 Tbsp water

1½ lb (680 g) boneless pork shoulder, trimmed of excess fat and cut into ½-inch (12-mm) thick slabs

SALAD

7 oz (200 g) thin rice vermicelli

2 cups (100 g) shredded green or napa cabbage

1 carrot, coarsely shredded

½ English cucumber, thinly sliced

1 cup (90 g) bean sprouts

¼ cup (3 g) fresh mint leaves, roughly torn

¼ cup (3 g) fresh cilantro leaves, roughly torn

¼ cup (30 g) chopped salted roasted peanuts

Nước Chấm (Vietnamese Dipping Sauce, page 44)

To marinate the pork, in a blender, combine the garlic, shallot, lemongrass, sugar, fish sauce, oil, soy sauce, and water and blend on medium speed, stopping and scraping down the sides of the blender as needed, until pureed. Put the pork into a medium baking dish or shallow bowl, pour the marinade evenly over the top, then turn the pork to coat evenly. Cover and refrigerate for at least 1 hour or up to 24 hours. Remove the pork from the refrigerator about 30 minutes before cooking to bring to room temperature.

To prepare the vermicelli, fill a bowl with hot water, add the noodles, and let soak until rehydrated and pliable, about 10 minutes, or according to package directions. Drain, rinse, and drain again.

To assemble the salad, divide the cabbage evenly among four shallow bowls. Divide the vermicelli evenly among the bowls, followed by the carrot, cucumber, and bean sprouts. Set aside.

To cook the pork, heat a large, heavy skillet over medium-high heat until very hot. Add a drizzle of oil. Remove the pork from the marinade, allowing any excess to drip off. Working in batches if needed to avoid crowding, add the pork to the skillet in a single layer and sear until well browned on the underside, then turn and continue to cook until the second side is well browned and the pork is just cooked through but still juicy, 7 to 9 minutes. Transfer the pork to a large plate. If working in batches, repeat with the remaining pork.

To serve, transfer the pork to a cutting board and let rest for a few minutes. Thinly slice the pork across the grain, divide evenly among the bowls, and then top with the mint, cilantro, and peanuts, dividing them evenly. Serve at once with the sauce alongside.

Nutrition Values (per serving): Energy (kJ) ~2552 kJ, Calories ~610 kcal, Fat ~22 g, Saturated Fat ~6 g, Carbohydrate ~58 g, Sugar ~9 g, Dietary Fiber ~5 g, Protein ~36 g, Cholesterol ~95 mg, Sodium ~1,200 mg

Crispy Chicken Milanese & Arugula Salad

The key to perfect chicken Milanese is butterflying the breasts into cutlets. This creates more surface area for the crispy, golden breadcrumbs and ensures the meat cooks quickly and evenly. Our fresh version is served over a lemony arugula salad and roasted yellow squash slices.

MAKES 4 SERVINGS

2 yellow squashes, sliced crosswise into rounds ¼ inch (6 mm) thick

Extra virgin olive oil, for drizzling

Kosher salt and freshly ground pepper

1 cup (60 g) panko breadcrumbs

4 small boneless, skinless chicken breasts (1½ lb/680 g)

2 tsp Italian seasoning

½ cup (120 g) sour cream

2 lemons

1 shallot, finely chopped

4 oz (115 g) baby arugula

8 oz (225 g) grape tomatoes, halved lengthwise (about 1⅓ cups)

To roast the squash, preheat the oven to 425°F (220°C). On a large sheet pan, toss the squash slices with a drizzle of oil, coating evenly, then season with salt and pepper. Spread the slices in a single layer. Roast, flipping the slices halfway through cooking, until lightly browned, 10 to 15 minutes. Set aside.

To prep the chicken, spread the breadcrumbs in a wide, shallow bowl. Have ready a large sheet pan. For each chicken breast, on a cutting board and holding it flat, use a sharp knife to cut horizontally through the breast from the thickest side. Keep the knife parallel to the board and stop about three-fourths of the way through the breast. Open each breast so it lies flat like a book and season all over with the Italian seasoning, salt, and pepper. One at a time, brush each cutlet with 2 Tbsp of the sour cream, then press the cutlet into the panko to coat completely and place on the sheet pan. Repeat with all the cutlets.

To cook the chicken, in a large nonstick skillet over medium-high heat, warm a generous drizzle of oil. Add the chicken cutlets in a single layer and cook, turning once, until golden brown on both sides and cooked through, 3 to 4 minutes on each side. Transfer to a cutting board.

To make the salad, cut the lemon in half, then cut half of the lemon into four wedges and reserve for serving. In a large bowl, whisk together the shallot, the juice from the remaining lemon half, and a generous drizzle of oil. Season with salt and pepper. Add the arugula and tomatoes and toss to coat evenly.

To assemble and serve, thinly slice the chicken cutlets across the grain. Divide the salad evenly among four plates and top with the squash. Top each serving with a sliced chicken cutlet and serve at once, with the lemon wedges to the side for squeezing over the top.

Nutrition Values (per serving): Energy (kJ) 2008 kJ, Calories 480 kcal, Fat 22 g, Saturated Fat 6 g, Carbohydrate 34 g, Sugar 10 g, Dietary Fiber 7 g, Protein 41 g, Cholesterol 125 mg, Sodium 260 mg

Chili-Lime Chicken & Veggie Salad with Peanut-Sambal Dressing

This Thai-inspired salad of chili-lime chicken, crisp snow peas, shredded cabbage, chopped romaine, toasted nuts and seeds, and a creamy, spicy peanut-based dressing crackles with fresh, zesty flavor. We top the finished salad with store-bought wonton strips for extra crunch, flavor, and fun.

MAKES 4 SERVINGS

PEANUT-SAMBAL DRESSING

½ cup (120 g) peanut sauce (page 133)

Juice of ½ lime

1 tsp sambal oelek or other chile paste

SALAD

6 oz (170 g) romaine lettuce hearts, chopped

2 cups (100 g) finely shredded green or red cabbage, or a mixture

1 cup (100 g) trimmed and thinly sliced snow peas

¼ cup shredded carrot

3 scallions, white and green parts, thinly sliced

3 cups (425 g) shredded cooked chicken (page 38)

Juice of ½ lime

1 tsp chili powder

Kosher salt

⅓ cup (35 g) sliced almonds, toasted

1 Tbsp toasted sesame seeds

Crispy wonton strips, for serving

To make the dressing, in a small bowl, whisk together the peanut sauce, lime juice, and sambal oelek, then taste and adjust with more sambal oelek if needed. The dressing should be thick but pourable. Thin with a little water if needed.

To make the salad, in a large salad bowl, combine the lettuce, cabbage, snow peas, carrot, and scallions and toss to mix. In a medium bowl, combine the chicken, lime juice, and chili powder and toss to mix. Season with salt. Add the chicken mixture to the lettuce mixture along with the almonds, sesame seeds, and half of the dressing and toss until all the ingredients are evenly coated. Top with the wonton strips and serve, passing the remaining dressing alongside.

Nutrition Values (per serving): Energy (kJ) ~2218 kJ, Calories ~530 kcal, Fat ~28 g, Saturated Fat ~5 g, Carbohydrate ~32 g, Sugar ~9 g, Dietary Fiber ~6 g, Protein ~36 g, Cholesterol ~85 mg, Sodium ~950 mg

Smoked Salmon Nicoise

A light tarragon vinaigrette brightens tender potatoes and crisp green beans in this simplified take on the classic Nicoise. Here, fresh tomatoes, cucumber, and briny Nicoise olives are topped with smoked salmon and boiled eggs for a salad that's elegant enough for company. If you like, switch out the smoked salmon for baked salmon fillets (page 40) or high-quality canned tuna.

MAKES 4 SERVINGS

TARRAGON VINAIGRETTE

¼ cup (60 ml) extra virgin olive oil

¼ cup (60 ml) vegetable oil

¼ cup (60 ml) white wine vinegar

1 Tbsp Dijon mustard

1 Tbsp minced shallot

1 Tbsp chopped fresh tarragon leaves

Pinch of sugar (optional)

Kosher salt and freshly ground pepper

SALAD

1 lb (450 g) yellow or red potatoes, unpeeled, cut into ¾-inch (2-cm) chunks

6 oz (170 g) thin green beans, preferably haricots verts, trimmed and halved crosswise

6 oz (170 g) baby lettuces or chopped butter lettuce leaves

Kosher salt and freshly ground pepper

8 oz (225 g) hot-smoked salmon, skinned and broken into chunks

8 oz (225 g) small ripe tomatoes, chopped, or cherry tomatoes

1 small English cucumber, sliced

¼ cup (40 g) pitted Niçoise olives

4 large eggs, boiled and peeled (see page 121)

To make the vinaigrette, in a jar, combine both oils, the vinegar, mustard, shallot, tarragon, and sugar (if using), cap tightly, and shake vigorously until well blended. Season with salt and pepper.

To cook the potatoes, fill a saucepan with salted water and bring to a boil over high heat. Fill a bowl with ice and water and set it near the stove. Add the potatoes to the boiling water and cook, stirring, until tender, about 10 minutes. Using a slotted spoon, transfer the potatoes to the ice bath until cold, then transfer them to a bowl.

To cook the green beans, add them to the boiling water and cook until bright green but crisp, about 2 minutes. Drain, then transfer to the ice bath until cold. Drain again and transfer to a bowl.

To dress the potatoes and green beans, drizzle the potatoes with about 3 Tbsp of the vinaigrette and the green beans with about 1 Tbsp of the vinaigrette. Season each bowl with salt and pepper and toss to coat.

To assemble the salad, add the lettuces to a bowl, drizzle with a little vinaigrette, season with salt and pepper, and toss to mix. Arrange the lettuces on a platter or divide among four plates. Top with the salmon, dressed potatoes, dressed green beans, tomatoes, cucumber, and olives, arranging them decoratively. Quarter the eggs and add to the platter or divide among the plates. Serve right away, passing the remaining vinaigrette at the table.

Nutrition Values (per serving): Energy (kJ) ~2176 kJ, Calories ~520 kcal, Fat ~32 g, Saturated Fat ~5 g, Carbohydrate ~26 g, Sugar ~4 g, Dietary Fiber ~5 g, Protein ~28 g, Cholesterol ~225 mg, Sodium ~1,100 mg

Chopped Carne Asada Salad

Bright, bold, citrus-marinated skirt steak meets crisp romaine, velvety avocado, fruity tomatoes, and tangy pickled jalapeños in this flavor-packed chopped salad. Tossed with zesty jalapeño ranch—one of our favorite dressings that we just can't get enough of—every bite pops.

MAKES 4 SERVINGS

CARNE ASADA

¼ cup (60 ml) fresh orange juice

2 Tbsp fresh lime juice

2 Tbsp olive oil

1 Tbsp *each* soy sauce, light brown sugar, and chili powder

¼ tsp granulated garlic

Kosher salt and ground pepper

1 lb (450 g) skirt steak, cut into four equal pieces

JALAPEÑO RANCH DRESSING

½ cup (120 g) mayonnaise

¼ cup (60 ml) buttermilk

3 scallions, chopped

¼ cup (10 g) chopped cilantro

1 jalapeño chile, seeded

Grated zest and juice of 1 lime

½ tsp *each* onion powder and garlic powder

SALAD

12 oz (340 g) romaine lettuce hearts, chopped

2 heirloom tomatoes, chopped

1 large ripe avocado, halved, pitted, peeled, and chopped

¼ red onion, finely chopped

¼ cup (30 g) sliced pickled jalapeño chiles, chopped

¼ cup (30 g) crumbled Cotija cheese or queso fresco

To marinate the carne asada, in a medium bowl, whisk together the orange juice, lime juice, oil, soy sauce, sugar, chili powder, and garlic until the sugar dissolves. Season the steak generously on both sides with salt and pepper. Put the steak into a shallow baking dish, pour the marinade evenly over the top, and then turn the steak to coat evenly. Cover and refrigerate for at least 1 hour or up to 24 hours. Remove the steak from the refrigerator about 30 minutes before grilling to bring to room temperature

To make the dressing, in a blender, combine the mayonnaise, buttermilk, scallions, cilantro, jalapeño, lime zest and juice, onion powder, garlic powder, and a pinch each of salt and pepper. Blend on medium speed until well mixed and smooth. Taste and adjust the seasoning with salt and pepper if needed. Transfer to an airtight container and refrigerate until ready to use. It will keep for up to 4 days.

To grill the steak, prepare a charcoal or gas grill for direct cooking over medium-high heat (450°F/230°C). When the grill is ready, brush the grill grates clean.

Remove the steak from the marinade, allowing any excess to drip off. Place the steak on the grill grates directly over the fire and grill, turning occasionally, until charred on both sides and cooked medium-rare, 5 to 7 minutes. Transfer to a cutting board and let rest for 5 minutes.

To assemble the salad, thinly slice the steak across the grain. In a large, wide bowl, combine the lettuce, tomatoes, avocado, onion, pickled jalapeños, and about three-fourths of the cheese. Drizzle with half of the dressing. Toss to coat all the ingredients evenly. Divide the salad among four shallow bowls. Top with the steak slices and sprinkle with the cheese, dividing evenly. Drizzle each with a little more dressing, then serve, with any remaining dressing alongside.

Nutrition Values (per serving): Energy (kJ) ~2678 kJ, Calories ~640 kcal, Fat ~38 g, Saturated Fat ~9 g, Carbohydrate ~28 g, Sugar ~7 g, Dietary Fiber ~8 g, Protein ~38 g, Cholesterol ~115 mg, Sodium ~1,050 mg

Summer Panzanella

Ripe tomatoes, sweet corn, crisp beans, toasted bread, and a simple vinaigrette are at the heart of this seasonal salad that's bursting with sunshine. Arugula adds a peppery accent, fresh mozzarella lends creaminess, and a mix of herbs brings brightness. Rustic, vibrant, and effortlessly fresh, this new spin on Tuscany's famed bread salad captures the essence of summer in a bowl.

MAKES 6 SERVINGS

VINAIGRETTE

¼ cup (60 ml) extra virgin olive oil

3 Tbsp red wine vinegar

1 tsp country Dijon mustard

½ tsp honey or agave nectar (optional)

Kosher salt and freshly ground pepper

SALAD

6 thick slices day-old country bread, crusts trimmed

Extra virgin olive oil, for brushing

Kosher salt and freshly ground pepper

2 cloves garlic, halved lengthwise

4 oz (115 g) mixed green beans and wax beans, trimmed and cut into 1-inch (2.5-cm) pieces

1 cup (130 g) corn kernels

2 large, ripe heirloom tomatoes, cut into bite-size pieces, or 2 cups (340 g) halved cherry tomatoes

3 cups (60 g) baby arugula

4 oz (115 g) fresh mozzarella cheese, cut into ½-inch (12-mm) pieces

¼ cup (30 g) very thinly sliced red onion

¼ cup (10 g) chopped mixed fresh herbs, such as basil, chives, and flat-leaf parsley

To make the vinaigrette, in a jar, combine the oil, vinegar, mustard, and honey, cap tightly, and shake vigorously until well blended. Season with salt and pepper.

To toast the bread, preheat the oven to 425°F (220°C). Arrange the bread in a single layer on a large sheet pan. Brush both sides of each slice lightly with oil, then season with a little salt and pepper. Bake, turning once about halfway through cooking, until crisp and golden brown, about 10 minutes. Remove from the oven and rub the bread with the cut sides of the garlic while still warm. Transfer to a cutting board and cut into 1-inch (2.5-cm) pieces. Transfer to a large salad bowl.

To blanch the beans and corn, fill a small saucepan half full with salted water and bring to a boil over high heat. Add the beans to the boiling water, turn down the heat to medium, and cook until tender-crisp, 1 to 3 minutes. When the beans are just tender-crisp, add the corn, then turn off the heat and let stand for 30 seconds. Drain into a colander and then hold under running cold water to halt the cooking. Drain well and transfer to the salad bowl.

To assemble the salad, add the tomatoes, arugula, mozzarella, onion, and herbs to the salad bowl and toss to mix well. Pour the vinaigrette over the top and toss gently to coat all the ingredients.

Serve at once, or set aside at room temperature for up to 1 hour before serving.

Nutrition Values (per serving): Energy (kJ) ~1506 kJ, Calories ~360 kcal, Fat ~18 g, Saturated Fat ~4 g, Carbohydrate ~38 g, Sugar ~6 g, Dietary Fiber ~4 g, Protein ~9 g, Cholesterol ~15 mg, Sodium ~480 mg

NO PESTICIDES
BROCCOLI
Plump Tomatoes

6 Family Favorites

"Dinner doesn't have to be complicated to feel special."

–Scott Fairbanks, HelloFresh Test Kitchen

There's a feeling you get when you walk into a kitchen and the smell instantly takes you back to childhood dinners, holiday gatherings, or just a simple, perfect weeknight supper. This is the chapter dedicated to those recipes: the family favorites that form the foundation of our happiest food memories.

At HelloFresh, we believe that the best meals are the ones shared with the people you love. They don't have to be complicated; they just need to be cooked with care and brimming with flavor. This collection is a celebration of that belief, featuring dishes that have stood the test of time, perfected by the home cooks who inspire us every day.

We've gathered comfort food classics and exciting new twists that are destined to become staples in your rotation. You'll find guaranteed weeknight wins like Spaghetti with Beef Ragù and the all-in-one deliciousness of Winner Winner Chicken Orzo Dinner. Looking for a weekend project? The celebratory Lebanese Stuffed Grape Leaves or the Argentine-inspired Chimichurri Steak & Potato Kebabs will make any meal feel special.

But this chapter isn't just about the classics. It's also about discovering the next generation of family favorites. Embrace global inspiration with the deeply satisfying Chile Beef Ramen Bowl, the street-food delight of Chicken Karaage, or the tangy bliss of Pickle-Brined Chicken Tenders. And for a fun, interactive dinner night, nothing beats a custom Pizza Party or serving up some nostalgic Detroit-Style Coney Dogs.

From Classic Beef Meat Loaf to the modern mash-up of Chile Crisp Salmon with Garlic Noodles, every recipe here is a promise: a full table, happy bellies, and moments of connection around great food. These are the dishes we return to again and again, the meals that make the kitchen the heart of the home.

So roll up your sleeves, gather your family, and get ready to cook the memories.

Pizza Party

Making pizza at home isn't just dinner, it's a full-on kitchen party! Roll out the dough, spread the sauce, and let everyone pile on toppings however they like, from classic pepperoni to wild vegetable combos. It's hands on, messy, and endlessly fun. We've gone with crowd-pleasers here—mushrooms, pepperoni, and red onion—but feel free to get creative.

MAKES TWO 12- TO 14-INCH (30- TO 36-CM) PIZZAS

DOUGH

1½ cups (360 ml) lukewarm water (105° to 115°F/40° to 46°C)

1 envelope (2¼ tsp) instant dry yeast

1 tsp sugar

4 cups (560 g) bread flour

2 tsp kosher salt

2 Tbsp olive oil

Semolina or bread flour, for dusting

PIZZA SAUCE

1 (15-oz/430-g) can crushed tomatoes

1 Tbsp extra virgin olive oil

1 tsp dried oregano

1 tsp kosher salt

½ tsp dried basil

½ tsp garlic powder

½ tsp sugar (optional)

Pinch of red pepper flakes (optional)

Freshly ground black pepper

To make the dough, in the bowl of a stand mixer, combine the water, yeast, and sugar and whisk to combine. Let sit for 5 minutes, then add the flour, salt, and oil. Fit the mixer with the dough hook and mix on low speed just until the ingredients come together. Increase the speed to medium and mix until a dough forms, pulls away from the sides of the bowl, and forms a smooth ball, about 7 minutes. If the dough is sticky, sprinkle in more flour, 1 tsp at a time, and continue to mix until it is only slightly tacky. If the dough is too dry and dry flour remains at the bottom of the bowl, add more water, 1 tsp at a time, and mix until the dough is evenly supple.

Transfer the dough to a floured work surface and knead until smooth and pliable, about 5 minutes. Divide the dough into two equal portions, shape each portion into a ball, and cover with a clean, damp kitchen towel or plastic wrap. Let rest until doubled in size, about 1 hour.

To make the pizza sauce, in a bowl, combine the tomatoes, oil, oregano, salt, basil, garlic powder, sugar (if using), red pepper flakes (if using), and a few grinds of black pepper. Stir, mixing well, and set aside.

Position an oven rack in the upper third of the oven and place a large pizza stone or pizza steel on the rack. Preheat the oven to 550°F (290°C) or as high as it will go for at least 30 minutes before baking the pizzas.

Make the toppings while the oven preheats. In a small skillet over medium heat, warm a drizzle of oil. Add the mushrooms and onion and season with salt and pepper. Cook, stirring, just until the vegetables are softened, about 6 minutes. Set aside.

continued . . .

Pizza Party

continued from page 154 . . .

TOPPINGS

Extra virgin olive oil, for cooking and brushing

1 cup (60 g) thinly sliced button or cremini mushrooms

½ cup (60 g) thinly sliced red onion

Kosher salt and freshly ground black pepper

1 cup (240 g) pizza sauce

12 oz (340 g) low-moisture mozzarella cheese, shredded on the large holes of a box grater-shredder

5 oz (140 g) sliced pepperoni

Fresh basil leaves, for garnish

To stretch the pizza dough, lightly dust a work surface with semolina. Transfer one dough portion to the dusted surface and gently press the dough into a thick disk. Using your hands or a tapered rolling pin, gently stretch or roll the dough into a round about ¼ inch (6 mm) thick and 12 to 14 inches (30 to 36 cm) in diameter, leaving a slightly thicker rim around the perimeter. Avoid overworking the dough, which can make it tough.

Dust a pizza peel generously with semolina. (An inverted baking sheet can stand in for a peel.) Transfer the stretched dough to the peel. Shake the peel gently to ensure the dough slides freely. If it sticks, lift the dough, add more semolina underneath, and gently reshape.

To top the pizza, brush the dough round lightly with oil. Spread ½ cup (120 g) of the pizza sauce over the dough in a thin layer, leaving a roughly 1-inch (2.5-cm) border. Sprinkle on half of the mozzarella, followed by half of the mushroom-onion mixture, distributing them evenly. Top with half of the pepperoni.

To bake the pizza, carefully slide the pizza from the peel onto the preheated stone or steel. Bake, rotating the pizza 180 degrees halfway through baking if your oven heats unevenly, until the crust is golden brown and the cheese is bubbly and lightly browned, 8 to 12 minutes. Use the pizza peel to transfer the pizza from the oven to a cutting board (or use a large metal spatula or tongs to gently ease the pizza onto the cutting board).

Garnish immediately with the basil leaves. Let the pizza rest for a few minutes before slicing and serving. Repeat with the remaining dough portion, sauce, and toppings to make the second pizza.

Nutrition Values (per serving for 6 servings): Energy (kJ) ~2230 kJ, Calories ~530 kcal, Fat ~25 g, Saturated Fat ~10 g, Carbohydrate ~57 g, Sugar ~5 g, Dietary Fiber ~3 g, Protein ~23 g, Cholesterol ~50 mg, Sodium ~970 mg

Tortellini Minestrone Soup

Minestrone is endlessly adaptable, making it easy to tailor to your family's tastes—or to clear out whatever's in the fridge. Toss in diced potatoes, chopped green beans, small broccoli florets, or handfuls of greens along with the onion mixture, adjusting the cooking time as needed. For a twist, swap the tortellini for ½ cup (55 g) of your favorite small pasta and use vegetable broth to keep the soup plant based.

MAKES 4 SERVINGS

2 Tbsp olive oil

½ yellow onion, finely chopped

1 large carrot, peeled and diced

1 large celery stalk celery, diced

Kosher salt and freshly ground pepper

1 (14-oz/400-g) can cannellini beans, drained and rinsed

1 (14-oz/400-g) can crushed tomatoes

1 small zucchini, diced

1 tsp Italian seasoning

3½ to 4 cups (830 to 950 ml) chicken or vegetable broth

1 (9- to 12-oz/255- to 340-g) package fresh or frozen cheese tortellini

¼ cup (60 g) basil pesto, homemade (page 43) or store-bought (optional)

Grated Parmesan cheese, for garnish

Crusty Italian or French bread, for serving

To make the soup, in a heavy soup pot over medium heat, warm the oil. Add the onion, carrot, celery, and a pinch of salt and cook, stirring, until the vegetables are tender, about 7 minutes. Add the beans, tomatoes, zucchini, Italian seasoning, 1 tsp salt, and a few grinds of pepper and stir to combine. Let simmer for 1 minute, then add 3½ cups (830 ml) of the broth and bring to a gentle boil. Turn down the heat to medium-low and simmer until the vegetables are tender, about 10 minutes. Taste and adjust the seasoning with salt and pepper if needed. Increase the heat to medium-high and bring the soup back to a boil.

Add the tortellini to the soup, stir well, and cook until the tortellini are al dente, according to the package directions. If the soup becomes too thick to your liking, add the remaining ½ cup (120 ml) broth.

To serve, ladle into soup bowls and garnish each bowl with a dollop of the pesto (if using) and plenty of Parmesan. Serve with the bread.

Nutrition Values (per serving): Energy (kJ) ~1757 kJ, Calories ~420 kcal, Fat ~14 g, Saturated Fat ~5 g, Carbohydrate ~56 g, Sugar ~8 g, Dietary Fiber ~8 g, Protein ~16 g, Cholesterol ~35 mg, Sodium ~1,150 mg

Buffalo Chicken Sliders

Pull, tear, and dig in—these flavor-packed sliders are made for family night. Soft, buttery pull-apart rolls cradle spicy shredded chicken, cooling celery slaw, and drizzles of blue cheese dressing, making every bite a little adventure. Perfect for sharing, piling high, and laughing over, they're finger-licking fun that turns dinner into a full-out party at the table. The slaw is best made and served at once, as it gets watery if it sits.

MAKES 4 TO 6 SERVINGS

TOASTED ROLLS

12-pack pull-apart slider rolls or dinner rolls

3 Tbsp unsalted butter, melted

1 Tbsp sesame seeds

CELERY SLAW

2 Tbsp mayonnaise

2 Tbsp sour cream

¼ cup (30 g) crumbled blue cheese

1 tsp white wine vinegar

2 cups (225 g) very thinly, diagonally sliced celery

2 Tbsp chopped fresh parsley

Kosher salt and freshly ground black pepper

BUFFALO CHICKEN

2 Tbsp unsalted butter

2⅓ cups (340 g) shredded cooked chicken (page 38)

¼ cup (60 ml) hot pepper sauce, preferably Crystal, plus more for serving

Kosher salt and freshly ground black pepper

Store-bought blue cheese dressing, for serving

Preheat the oven to 400°F (200°C).

To toast the rolls, using a large serrated knife, split the rolls in half horizontally. Arrange the roll halves cut-side up on a sheet pan and lightly brush the cut sides with about 2 Tbsp of the butter. Turn the roll tops cut-side down and brush the tops with the remaining 1 Tbsp butter. Sprinkle the roll tops with the sesame seeds.

Bake until the cut sides are toasted, 4 to 6 minutes depending on the type of rolls. Remove from the oven and transfer the roll bottoms cut-side up to a serving platter.

To make the celery slaw, in a bowl, stir together the mayonnaise, sour cream, blue cheese, and vinegar, mixing well. Add the celery and parsley and stir and toss to coat. Season with salt and black pepper.

To make the Buffalo chicken, in a medium skillet over medium heat, melt the butter. Add the chicken and hot sauce and cook, stirring and tossing, until the chicken is coated with the sauce and warmed through, about 2 minutes. Season with salt and pepper.

To fill the sliders, using tongs, transfer the chicken to the roll bottoms, spreading it in an even layer. Top with the celery slaw, dividing it evenly, then close the sliders with the roll tops, cut-side down.

Serve at once, with more hot sauce and the blue cheese dressing alongside for dipping.

Nutrition Values (per serving for 6 servings): Energy (kJ) ~2600 kJ, Calories ~620 kcal, Fat ~34 g, Saturated Fat ~13 g, Carbohydrate ~52 g, Sugar ~8 g, Dietary Fiber ~3 g, Protein ~27 g, Cholesterol ~105 mg, Sodium ~1,050 mg

Chile Crisp Salmon with Garlic Noodles

Sweet, spicy, and bursting with flavor, this dish pairs salmon glazed with honey and chile crisp with garlicky noodles that soak up every bit of sauce. The noodles are buttery, savory, and satisfyingly rich, while the salmon delivers a punch of heat tempered by the flavor of lemon. Serve with stir-fried bok choy or broccolini (page 54) .

MAKES 4 SERVINGS

GARLIC NOODLES

3 Tbsp unsalted butter

3 scallions, white and green parts, thinly sliced and parts kept separate

6 garlic cloves, minced

2 Tbsp oyster sauce

2 Tbsp soy sauce

1 Tbsp honey

1 Tbsp chile crisp

2 tsp Asian fish sauce

12 oz (340 g) spaghetti or linguine

GLAZED SALMON

4 Tbsp (55 g) unsalted butter, at room temperature

2 Tbsp chile crisp

1 Tbsp honey

Finely grated zest and juice of 1 lemon

4 skinless salmon fillets (about 6 oz/170 g each), pin bones removed

Kosher salt

Preheat the oven to 425°F (220°C). Fill a large saucepan three-fourths full with salted water and bring to a boil over high heat.

To make the sauce for the noodles, in a large skillet over medium-low heat, melt the butter. Add the scallion whites and garlic and cook, stirring, until fragrant, about 1 minute. Add the oyster sauce, soy sauce, honey, chile crisp, and fish sauce and mix well. Remove from the heat and set aside.

To make the salmon, in a small bowl, combine the butter, chile crisp, honey, and lemon zest and juice. Using a fork, mash and stir the ingredients together until a well-blended paste forms. Arrange the salmon fillets in a single layer on a small sheet pan or in a medium baking dish. Sprinkle the salmon with salt, then spread the butter mixture on top of the fillets, dividing it evenly.

Bake until the thickest part of a fillet is just cooked through (barely opaque and still moist) and flakes easily with a fork, 10 to 14 minutes, depending on the thickness of the fillet. Avoid overcooking.

While the salmon is baking, add the spaghetti to the boiling water and cook, stirring occasionally, until al dente, about 10 minutes or according to package directions. Reserve a little pasta cooking water.

Using tongs, transfer the spaghetti to the skillet with the sauce and place over medium heat. Cook, stirring and tossing with the tongs, until the noodles are well coated and the sauce is hot, about 2 minutes. Add a little pasta cooking water to loosen the sauce if you like.

To serve, divide the noodles among four shallow bowls and top each with a salmon fillet. Garnish with the scallion greens and serve at once.

Nutrition Values (per serving): Energy (kJ) ~3013 kJ, Calories ~720 kcal, Fat ~32 g, Saturated Fat ~14 g, Carbohydrate ~68 g, Sugar ~10 g, Dietary Fiber ~3 g, Protein ~36 g, Cholesterol ~95 mg, Sodium ~1,450 mg

Spiced Turkey Meatball Pita Pockets

Laced with fragrant herbs and spices, these turkey meatballs are stuffed into pita pockets along with a simple romaine salad, feta, and a dollop of Greek yogurt for a quick and satisfying dinner. The meatballs are just as at home in pasta, grain bowls, salads, or even served solo with a dipping sauce. For an Italian-style meatball, replace the cumin and cinnamon with Italian seasoning.

MAKES 4 SERVINGS

TURKEY MEATBALLS

1 Tbsp vegetable oil
½ yellow onion, finely chopped
1 cup (40 g) fresh breadcrumbs
3 Tbsp whole milk
1 large egg, beaten
½ medium carrot, finely shredded
1 Tbsp chopped fresh parsley
1 Tbsp finely chopped cilantro
2 tsp finely chopped fresh mint
½ tsp ground cumin
½ tsp kosher salt
½ tsp freshly ground pepper
¼ tsp ground cinnamon
1 lb (450 g) ground turkey

PITA POCKETS

½ cup (120 g) plain Greek yogurt
2 scallions, white and green parts, finely chopped
5 oz (140 g) romaine lettuce, chopped
1 cup (170 g) halved cherry tomatoes
2 Persian cucumbers, thinly sliced
½ cup (60 g) crumbled feta
½ lemon
Kosher salt and freshly ground pepper
4 pita breads, halved and toasted

Preheat the oven to 450°F (230°C).

To make the meatballs, in a skillet over medium heat, warm the oil. Add the onion and cook, stirring, until golden brown, 5 to 8 minutes. Let cool slightly then transfer to a large bowl. Add the breadcrumbs and milk and mix well. Add the egg, carrot, parsley, cilantro, mint, cumin, salt, pepper, and cinnamon and stir until well mixed. Add the turkey and mix gently until the mixture is well combined.

Grease a large sheet pan with oil. For each meatball, scoop up about 2 Tbsp of the meat mixture (a cookie scoop works well for this), form into a ball, and set on the prepared sheet pan. You should have about sixteen meatballs. (The meatballs can be made, covered, and refrigerated up to a day in advance of cooking.)

To roast the meatballs, place in the oven and roast, turning once halfway through cooking, until nicely browned and cooked through, about 15 minutes. Set aside.

While the meatballs roast, prepare the pocket fillings. In a bowl, stir together the yogurt and scallions. In another bowl, toss together the lettuce, tomatoes, cucumbers, and feta. Squeeze the lemon half over the salad, season with salt and pepper, and toss to mix.

To assemble and serve, gently open each pita half to create a pocket. Stuff two meatballs into each pita pocket (you may need to cut them in half so they fit), then divide the salad evenly among the pockets. Add a small dollop of the yogurt sauce to each pocket and serve. Pass the remaining yogurt sauce at the table.

Nutrition Values (per serving): Energy (kJ) ~2343 kJ, Calories ~560 kcal, Fat ~24 g, Saturated Fat ~8 g, Carbohydrate ~48 g, Sugar ~6 g, Dietary Fiber ~5 g, Protein ~34 g, Cholesterol ~115 mg, Sodium ~1,050 mg

Detroit-Style Coney Dogs

Madeline Jerge from our Product Operations team grew up in Detroit, Michigan, where Coney dogs are a summertime staple. Inspired by the chili-topped dogs served at the city's famed hot dog diner, Lafayette Coney Island, this recipe calls for the meat topping to be cooked down until almost paste-like and finished with classic yellow mustard—no Dijon allowed. Every bite delivers the familiar, comforting flavors of home, making these hearty, messy hot dogs a nostalgic favorite for anyone who craves the legendary Detroit specialty.

MAKES 6 CONEY DOGS

Vegetable oil, for drizzling
8 oz (225 g) ground beef
5 Tbsp (85 g) tomato paste
1½ tsp kosher salt
1½ tsp chili powder
1½ tsp Worcestershire sauce
½ tsp freshly ground pepper
2 cups (475 ml) water
6 hot dogs
6 hot dog buns, split and toasted
Yellow mustard, for serving
Diced yellow onion, for serving

To make the chili, in a small skillet or saucepan over medium heat, warm a drizzle of oil. Add the ground beef and cook, stirring and breaking up the meat with a wooden spoon, until browned, about 5 minutes. Stir in the tomato paste, mixing well, then season with the salt, chili powder, Worcestershire, and pepper. Pour in the water and mix well.

Bring the mixture to a boil, then reduce the heat to low and simmer, stirring occasionally and continuing to break up the meat, until the chili thickens, about 45 minutes.

To boil the hot dogs, fill a large pot half full of water and bring to a boil over medium-high heat. Add the hot dogs and cook until plump and heated through, 4 to 6 minutes. Using tongs, transfer to paper towels to blot off any excess moisture.

To grill the hot dogs, prepare a charcoal or gas grill for direct cooking over medium-high heat (450°F/230°C). When the grill is ready, brush the grill grates clean. Grill the hot dogs over the fire, turning occasionally, until plump, browned, and heated through, 5 to 7 minutes.

To serve, place a hot dog in each bun, then top with the chili, dividing evenly. Garnish with onions and a drizzle of mustard and serve at once.

Nutrition Values (per Coney dog): Energy (kJ) ~1715 kJ, Calories ~410 kcal, Fat ~22 g, Saturated Fat ~8 g, Carbohydrate ~32 g, Sugar ~6 g, Dietary Fiber ~2 g, Protein ~16 g, Cholesterol ~55 mg, Sodium ~1,150 mg

Winner Winner Chicken Orzo Dinner

Although the zucchini and tomato medley starts as a side, it quickly steals the spotlight. Crispy panko, melty mozzarella, and Parmesan create a perfect balance of crunch and creaminess. Paired with herbed chicken and bright, lemony orzo, this Top 10 Hall of Fame recipe proves that a family dinner can be light, satisfying, and full of standout flavor—especially when vegetables take center stage.

MAKES 4 SERVINGS

2 zucchini, cut into rounds ¼ inch (6 mm) thick

2 Roma tomatoes, cut into wedges ½ inch (12 mm) thick

Olive oil, for drizzling

2 Tbsp Italian seasoning

Kosher salt and freshly ground pepper

1 cup (6 oz/170 g) orzo

4 small boneless, skinless chicken breasts (1½ lb/680 g)

½ cup (30 g) panko breadcrumbs

8 oz (225 g) fresh mozzarella cheese, cut into ½-inch (12-mm) cubes

½ cup (15 g) grated Parmesan cheese

1 lemon, halved

3 Tbsp chopped fresh flat-leaf parsley

Position an oven rack in the upper third of the oven and preheat the oven to 425°F (220°C).

To roast the vegetables, pile the zucchini and tomatoes on a large sheet pan. Drizzle with oil and season with 1 Tbsp of the Italian seasoning and with salt and pepper. Toss to coat evenly, then spread in an even layer.

Roast the vegetables, stirring once or twice, until tender, about 10 minutes.

Meanwhile, cook the orzo. Fill a medium saucepan three-fourths full with salted water and bring to a boil over high heat. Add the orzo, bring the water back to a boil, and cook, stirring occasionally, until al dente, about 7 minutes or according to package directions. Drain well in a colander, then return to the pan and cover to keep warm.

To prep the chicken, place a chicken breast on a cutting board and hold it flat with your nondominant hand. With a sharp knife, and starting from the thickest side, cut horizontally through the breast, keeping the knife parallel to the board and stopping about three-fourths of the way through the breast. Repeat with the remaining chicken breasts. Open each breast so it lies flat like a book and season all over with the remaining 1 Tbsp Italian seasoning and with salt and pepper.

To cook the chicken, in a large nonstick skillet over medium-high heat, warm a generous drizzle of oil. When the oil is shimmering, add the chicken in a single layer and cook, turning once, until lightly browned on both sides and just cooked through, 3 to 4 minutes on each side. Transfer to a large plate.

continued . . .

Winner Winner Chicken Orzo Dinner

continued from page 177 . . .

To finish the vegetables, when they are tender-crisp, remove from the oven and set the sheet pan aside. Increase the oven temperature to 500°F (260°F) or turn off the oven and turn on the broiler.

Sprinkle the vegetables evenly with the panko, mozzarella, and Parmesan. Return the vegetables to the oven and roast or broil until the breadcrumbs are golden brown, the cheese is melted, and the vegetables are tender, 3 to 5 minutes.

To finish the orzo, squeeze the juice from half of the lemon into the pan, then stir in half of the parsley. Season with salt and pepper and stir again. Cut the remaining lemon half into quarters.

To serve, divide the orzo evenly among four plates. Top with the vegetables and the chicken, dividing them evenly among the plates. Drizzle with any accumulated juices from the plate that held the chicken. Garnish each plate with one-fourth of the remaining parsley and a lemon wedge and serve.

Nutrition Values (per serving): Energy (kJ) 3054 kJ, Calories 730 kcal, Fat 33 g, Saturated Fat 15 g, Carbohydrate 54 g, Sugar 8 g, Dietary Fiber 7 g, Protein 61 g, Cholesterol 160 mg, Sodium 520 mg

Spaghetti with Beef Ragù

This dish has been a family favorite for generations. Friend of HelloFresh Sarah Voss grew up eating it weekly. Her dad learned how to make it from his mother, who got the recipe from a Sicilian woman in Germany. When Sarah lived in South Korea, her dad would fly in and buy every ingredient to make it for her. Even after his passing, the rich sauce and comforting flavors bring back fond memories of family, love, and home. According to Sarah, it's best served with a side of Garlic Bread (page 55).

MAKES 4 TO 6 SERVINGS

Olive oil, for drizzling

8 oz (225 g) cremini or button mushrooms, trimmed and finely chopped

Kosher salt and freshly ground pepper

1 small yellow onion, diced

1 lb (450 g) ground beef (85 percent lean)

1 Tbsp dried oregano

1 (6-oz/170-g) can tomato paste

2 or 3 garlic cloves, minced

1 (28-oz/900-g) can whole or diced tomatoes, with juices

1 lb (450 g) spaghetti

Grated Parmesan cheese, for serving

To make the meat sauce, in a large pot over medium-high heat, warm a generous drizzle of oil. Add the mushrooms and a pinch of salt and cook, stirring occasionally, until they release their liquid and brown, 6 to 8 minutes. Transfer to a bowl.

Reduce the heat to medium and add another drizzle of oil to the pot. Add the onion and cook, stirring, until golden, 5 to 7 minutes. Add the beef and cook, stirring and breaking up the meat with a wooden spoon, until browned, about 5 minutes.

Stir in the oregano until fragrant, then add the tomato paste and cook, stirring, until it darkens, about 3 minutes. Stir in the garlic until fragrant, then add the canned tomatoes and juices, crushing whole tomatoes with your hands if using. Stir in the reserved mushrooms. Bring the mixture to a gentle boil, then turn down the heat to low, cover, and simmer, stirring occasionally, until the ragu is thick and richly flavored, at least 1½ hours and up to 4 hours.

To cook the spaghetti, when the sauce is ready, fill a large pot three-fourths full with salted water and bring to a boil over high heat. Add the spaghetti and cook, stirring occasionally, until al dente, about 10 minutes or according to package instructions. Drain the pasta.

To serve, divide the spaghetti evenly among plates or shallow bowls. Top each portion with a generous amount of the sauce and sprinkle with Parmesan. Serve at once. (You will not need all the sauce. Store the remaining sauce in an airtight container in the refrigerator for up to 4 days or freeze for up to 3 months.)

Nutrition Values (per serving for 6 servings): Energy (kJ) ~2900 kJ, Calories ~490 kcal, Fat ~22 g, Saturated Fat ~8 g, Carbohydrate ~86 g, Sugar ~11 g, Dietary Fiber ~6 g, Protein ~34 g, Cholesterol ~95 mg, Sodium ~620 mg

Lebanese Stuffed Grape Leaves

These stuffed grape leaves carry generations of family tradition. Madeline Jerge, a member of our Product Operations team, grew up with a grandfather from Lebanon, and the grape leaves made by his sisters were always her favorite dish at family gatherings. Today, her mother, Mary Ann, keeps the tradition alive with these seasoned lamb-and-rice rolls. If you cannot source fresh grape leaves, purchase jarred grape leaves in brine. Drain the leaves, rinse well under cold running water, then drain well in a colander. Snip off the stems before stuffing.

MAKES 8 TO 10 SERVINGS; ABOUT 34 STUFFED GRAPE LEAVES

½ cup (100 g) medium-grain white rice

4 Tbsp (55 g) unsalted butter, melted

¼ tsp ground cinnamon

¼ tsp kosher salt

¼ tsp freshly ground pepper

8 oz (225 g) ground lamb

40 fresh grape leaves, excess stems trimmed

3 or 4 thin bone-in pork loin chops (about 1½ lb/680g total weight)

1½ cups (360 ml) chicken broth

½ cup (60 ml) fresh lemon juice (about 3 lemons)

To make the filling, in a bowl, combine the rice, butter, cinnamon, salt, and pepper and stir until blended. Add the lamb and mix thoroughly.

To blanch the grape leaves, bring a large pot three-fourths of water to a boil over high heat. Add the grape leaves and simmer until softened, 1 to 2 minutes. Drain.

To stuff the grape leaves, place a grape leaf, textured side up and stem end near you, on a work surface. Spoon about 2 Tbsp of the filling onto the center of the leaf, fold the sides in over the filling, and, starting at the stem end, roll up the leaf around the filling. Set aside seam-side down. Repeat until all the filling is used. You should have about 34 stuffed grape leaves.

To cook the stuffed grape leaves, line the bottom of a large pot with the pork chops. Cover the pork chops with a layer of grape leaves. Arrange the stuffed grape leaves, seam side down, in rows on top of the leaves, stacking them on top of one another. Place a heatproof plate on top of the top row of stuffed grape leaves so they won't float as they are cooking. Pour the broth and lemon juice into the pot.

Cover the pot, place over medium heat, and bring the liquid to a boil. Turn down the heat to low and simmer gently until the rice is tender and the lamb is cooked through, 1 to 1½ hours; you can test one by removing it and cutting it in half to make sure the lamb is cooked through. Remove the plate and drain any excess liquid from the pot, then set aside for about 30 minutes to cool.

Transfer the stuffed grape leaves to a platter and serve.

Nutrition Values (per 6 stuffed grape leaves): Energy (kJ) ~980 kJ, Calories ~235 kcal, Fat ~23 g, Saturated Fat ~8 g, Carbohydrate ~18 g, Sugar ~1 g, Dietary Fiber ~1 g, Protein ~8 g, Cholesterol ~55 mg, Sodium ~225 mg

Classic Beef Meat Loaf

Every time Culinary Team member Sara Heilman visits her family in Iowa, she requests her mother's classic meat loaf. A quintessential Midwest comfort meal, it pairs perfectly with buttery mashed potatoes (page 51) and fresh—or even frozen—green beans. Each bite evokes the kind of old-school nostalgia and satisfaction that every memorable home-cooked meal brings to the table. Use your favorite barbecue sauce in place of the ketchup if desired.

MAKES 4 SERVINGS

1 lb (450 g) ground beef (85 percent lean)

½ cup (70 g) diced yellow onion

½ cup (130 g) ketchup, plus ¼ cup (65 g) for spreading on top of the loaf

20 saltines, crushed

1 large egg, beaten

1 Tbsp Worcestershire sauce

1 tsp kosher salt

½ tsp freshly ground pepper

Preheat the oven to 350°F (175°C). Lightly oil a baking sheet or a wide 2-qt (1.9-L) baking dish.

To make the meat loaf, in a large bowl, combine the beef, onion, the ½ cup (70 g) ketchup, the saltines, egg, Worcestershire sauce, salt, and pepper. Gently mix with your hands until all the ingredients are well blended.

Mound the meat mixture on the prepared sheet pan, then shape into a loaf about 2 inches (5 cm) tall. Spread the remaining ¼ cup (65 g) ketchup evenly over the top.

Bake the meat loaf until browned and an instant-read thermometer inserted into the center of the loaf registers 160°F (71°C), 50 to 60 minutes. Let rest for 5 minutes before serving.

To serve, cut into thick slices.

Nutrition Values (per serving): Energy (kJ) ~1620KJ , Calories ~390 kcal, Fat ~20 g, Saturated Fat ~7 g, Carbohydrate ~26 g, Sugar ~12 g, Dietary Fiber ~0.6 g, Protein ~24 g, Cholesterol ~124 mg, Sodium ~1265 mg

Chimichurri Steak & Potato Kebabs

Chimichurri, an herb-forward sauce from Argentina, is traditionally served with grilled meats for good reason. Its fresh, tangy, slightly spicy flavors cut through the richness while enhancing the meats' natural flavor. Here, it's the perfect match for beef and potato kebabs cooked over a fire.

MAKES 4 TO 6 SERVINGS

STEAK KEBABS

3 Tbsp Worcestershire sauce

1 Tbsp country Dijon mustard

1 Tbsp olive oil, plus more for brushing

3 garlic cloves, minced

1 tsp plus 1 Tbsp kosher salt

½ tsp freshly ground black pepper

1½ lb (680 g) boneless beef chuck roast, trimmed of excess fat and cut into 1-inch (2.5-cm) chunks

1 lb (450 g) small red potatoes, unpeeled, cut into 1½-inch (4-cm) chunks

1 red onion, cut into 1½-inch (4-cm) pieces

CHIMICHURRI

1 cup (40 g) packed chopped fresh flat-leaf parsley

2 Tbsp chopped fresh oregano leaves

2 garlic cloves, minced

6 Tbsp (90 ml) extra-virgin olive oil

¼ cup (60 ml) red wine vinegar

½ tsp red pepper flakes (optional)

Kosher salt and freshly ground black pepper

To marinate the steak, in a bowl, whisk together the Worcestershire sauce, mustard, oil, garlic, 1 tsp of the salt, and the black pepper. Add the beef and toss to coat. Cover and refrigerate for 30 minutes.

To make the chimichurri, in a food processor, combine the parsley, oregano, garlic, oil, vinegar, and red pepper flakes (if using) and pulse until finely chopped and well combined, stopping to scrape down the sides of the bowl as needed. Season with salt and black pepper. Transfer to a small bowl and set aside. The chimichurri can be made up to 1 day in advance and refrigerated in an airtight container.

To parboil the potatoes, in a saucepan, combine the potatoes with water to cover and 1 Tbsp salt. Bring to a boil over high heat, turn down the heat to medium, and boil gently until just barely tender, about 8 minutes. Drain, rinse under cold running water, and drain again.

Prepare a charcoal or gas grill for direct cooking over medium-high heat (450°F/230°C). When the grill is ready, brush the grill grates clean.

While the grill is heating, assemble the kebabs. Remove the beef from the marinade, allowing any excess to drip off. Thread the beef, potato, and onion pieces onto metal skewers, alternating them on the skewers. (Bamboo skewers can be used if soaked in water to cover for 30 minutes before using.) Brush the kebabs all over with a little oil.

To grill the kebabs, arrange the skewers on the grill grates directly over the fire and grill, turning a few times, until charred on all sides and the beef is done to your liking, about 8 minutes for medium-rare. Transfer the kebabs to a serving platter and let rest for 5 minutes before serving.

To serve, spoon some of the chimichurri over the kebabs, then serve the remaining chimichurri alongside.

Nutrition Values (per serving for 6 servings): Energy (kJ) ~2430 kJ, Calories ~580 kcal, Fat ~30 g, Saturated Fat ~10 g, Carbohydrate ~22 g, Sugar ~4 g, Dietary Fiber ~3 g, Protein ~36 g, Cholesterol ~110 mg, Sodium ~820 mg

Spiced Lamb Burgers with Tomato Chutney

These lamb burgers are full of flavor, and the sweet-tangy tomato chutney adds a bright, layered contrast. The recipe makes more chutney than you need for the burgers, but it's great on lots of things (try it with the turkey meatballs on page 173). Or you can skip the chutney and spread the burgers with hummus, tzatziki (page 218), or a fresh mint or cilantro chutney.

MAKES 4 BURGERS

TOMATO CHUTNEY

2 Tbsp olive oil

1½ tsp yellow mustard seeds

¼ cup (35 g) finely chopped yellow onion

Kosher salt

¼ cup (60 ml) apple cider vinegar

¼ cup (50 g) light brown sugar

½ tsp ground ginger

¼ tsp garlic powder

¼ tsp ground cinnamon

1 (14½-oz/415-g) can crushed tomatoes

1 Tbsp fresh lemon juice

BURGERS

1½ lb (680 g) ground lamb

3 Tbsp finely chopped onion

1 Tbsp finely chopped fresh mint and/or flat-leaf parsley

1 tsp kosher salt

1 tsp ground cumin

½ tsp paprika

½ tsp freshly ground pepper

¼ tsp garlic powder

4 large slices Havarti cheese

4 burger buns, split and toasted

1 cup (50 g) shredded romaine lettuce

To make the tomato chutney, in a small saucepan over medium-low heat, warm the oil. Add the mustard seeds, then add the onion and a pinch of salt. Cook, stirring, until the onion softens, about 5 minutes. Stir in the vinegar, sugar, ginger, garlic powder, cinnamon, and 1 tsp salt, then add the tomatoes and mix well. Bring to a simmer and cook, stirring often, until the mixture thickens, about 10 minutes. Remove from the heat and stir in the lemon juice. Taste adjust the seasoning with salt and lemon juice if needed. Set aside to cool. (The chutney can be stored in an airtight container in the refrigerator for up to 2 weeks or in the freezer for up to 3 months.)

To make the lamb patties, in a large bowl, combine the lamb, onion, mint, salt, cumin, paprika, pepper, and garlic powder. Using your hands, mix gently until all the ingredients are well blended. Divide the mixture into four equal portions. Gently roll each portion into a ball, then flatten into a patty about ½ inch (12 mm) thick. Place the patties on a plate.

To grill the lamb patties, prepare a charcoal or gas grill for direct cooking over medium-high heat (450°F/230°C). When the grill is ready, brush the grill grates clean. Arrange the patties on the grill grates directly over the fire and grill until nicely etched with grill marks on the underside, about 3 minutes. Turn and grill until nicely etched with grill marks on the second side, about 3 minutes. Flip once more, add the cheese slices to the patties, and close the lid. Cook until the cheese melts and the burgers are done to your liking, 1 to 2 minutes longer for medium-well.

To serve, transfer the patties to the bun bottoms. Top each patty with some of the chutney and one-fourth of the lettuce. Close with the bun tops and serve at once.

Nutrition Values (per burger): Energy (kJ) ~3013 kJ, Calories ~720 kcal, Fat ~38 g, Saturated Fat ~16 g, Carbohydrate ~48 g, Sugar ~10 g, Dietary Fiber ~3 g, Protein ~38 g, Cholesterol ~125 mg, Sodium ~1,150 mg

Chile Beef Ramen Bowl

This recipe takes inspiration from the bold, chile-rich flavors found in Mexican beef birria and pairs them with the cozy ease of instant ramen for a family-friendly weeknight mash-up. The slow-cooked beef, which simmers in a smoky, spicy sauce that hints at birria's depth, is also excellent served over steamed rice or as a stew with warm tortillas alongside.

MAKES 4 TO 6 SERVINGS

CHILE BEEF RAMEN

2½ lb (1.1 kg) boneless beef chuck, cut into 1½- to 2-inch pieces

Kosher salt and freshly ground pepper

Vegetable oil, for cooking

1 medium yellow onion, chopped

4 garlic cloves, chopped

1 (14.5-oz/415-g) can diced fire-roasted tomatoes, with juices

1 oz (30 g) guajillo chiles (2 or 3), seeded and roughly chopped

1½ cups (360 ml) water

2 cups (475 ml) beef or chicken broth

3 Tbsp apple cider vinegar

2 Tbsp chopped chipotle chiles in adobo (seeded if desired), plus 1 Tbsp adobo sauce

2 tsp dried oregano, preferably Mexican

1 tsp ground cumin

1 tsp smoked paprika

1 tsp sugar

1 cinnamon stick

2 bay leaves

1 star anise pod

4 to 6 packages (each 4 ounces/115 g) instant ramen noodles, seasoning packets removed

To brown the meat, season the beef pieces generously all over with salt and pepper. In a large Dutch oven over medium-high heat, drizzle a generous amount of oil. When the oil is shimmering, add half of the beef and sear without turning until richly browned on the underside, about 3 minutes. Turn and sear the second side until browned, about 3 minutes. Transfer to a large plate and repeat with the remaining beef.

To make the sauce, turn down the heat to medium and add the onion to the pot. Cook, stirring and scraping up any browned bits on the pot bottom, until the onion is tender and starting to brown, about 4 minutes. Add the garlic and cook, stirring, until fragrant, about 1 minute. Add the tomatoes and juices, guajillo chiles, and water and stir well. Bring to a gentle boil, then turn down the heat to low, cover, and simmer until the chiles are softened, about 10 minutes.

Transfer the guajillo chile mixture to a blender and add the broth, vinegar, chipotle chiles, adobo sauce, oregano, cumin, paprika, sugar, 1 tsp salt, and ½ tsp pepper and blend on medium speed until completely smooth.

To braise the beef, pour the pureed chile mixture into the Dutch oven and add the seared beef, cinnamon stick, bay leaves, and star anise. Bring to a simmer over medium heat, then turn down the heat to low, cover partially, and simmer gently, stirring occasionally, until the beef is very tender, about 1½ hours. Remove from the heat.

Using a slotted spoon, transfer the beef to a cutting board and shred with two forks. Scoop out the bay leaves, cinnamon stick, and star anise from the pot and discard. Return the beef to the pot, and stir to mix. If you prefer a looser sauce, thin with water to the consistency you like. Taste and adjust the seasoning with salt, pepper, and vinegar if needed.

continued . . .

"Cooking at home is an act of love made visable on the plate."

–Adam Kalikow

Chile Beef Ramen Bowl

continued from page 186 . . .

To boil the ramen, fill a large saucepan half full with salted water and bring to a boil over high heat. Add the ramen and cook, stirring often, until tender, about 4 minutes or according to package directions. Drain into a colander.

To assemble and serve, while the ramen cooks, return the braised beef to medium-low heat to gently warm. Divide the ramen evenly among four to six bowls. Ladle a generous amount of the braised beef over the noodles in each bowl. Top each serving with the white onion, scallions, and pickled jalapeño (if using), dividing them evenly. Garnish each bowl with a sprinkle of cilantro and a lime wedge and serve at once.

TOPPINGS

½ small white onion, finely chopped

3 scallions, white and green parts, thinly sliced

¼ cup (30 g) pickled jalapeño slices (optional)

Chopped fresh cilantro

1 large lime, cut into four to six wedges

Nutrition Values (per serving for 6 servings): Energy (kJ) ~2552 kJ, Calories ~610 kcal, Fat ~24 g, Saturated Fat ~9 g, Carbohydrate ~58 g, Sugar ~6 g, Dietary Fiber ~5 g, Protein ~38 g, Cholesterol ~95 mg, Sodium ~1,450 mg

Pickle-Brined Chicken Tenders

Pickling isn't just for cucumbers. These chicken tenders get a bright, tangy kick from a quick dunk in pickle juice. Coated in panko for a golden, crispy crust, they're perfect for dipping into jalapeño ranch, honey mustard, or barbecue sauce. If chicken tenders aren't available, cut boneless, skinless chicken breasts into strips about 2 inches (5 cm) wide and 4 to 5 inches (10 to 13 cm) long for this playful, hands-on meal that's sure to please kids and adults alike.

MAKES 4 SERVINGS

1½ lb (680 g) chicken tenders

Kosher salt and freshly ground pepper

½ cup (120 ml) dill pickle juice

½ cup (70 g) all-purpose flour

⅓ cup (80 ml) buttermilk

1 large egg

1½ cups (90 g) panko breadcrumbs

Vegetable oil, for frying

Jalapeño ranch dressing (see Chopped Carne Asada Salad, page 156), honey mustard, or barbecue sauce, for dipping

To marinate the chicken, put the chicken into a medium shallow bowl or baking dish and season all over with salt and pepper. Pour the pickle juice over the chicken and stir to coat. Cover and refrigerate for 30 minutes or up to 4 hours.

To coat the chicken, line up three wide, shallow small bowls. In the first bowl, whisk together the flour, ½ tsp salt, and ½ tsp pepper. In the second bowl, whisk together the buttermilk and egg. Add the breadcrumbs to the third bowl. Have ready a large sheet pan.

Pour off the pickle juice and pat the chicken dry. One at a time, dredge the chicken pieces in the flour mixture, coating evenly and shaking off the excess, then dip in the buttermilk mixture, turning to coat and letting the excess drip off. Finally, dredge each piece in the breadcrumbs, coating evenly and pressing the crumbs to adhere, then set aside on the sheet pan. Repeat until all the chicken tenders are coated.

To cook the chicken, pour oil to a depth of ½ inch (12 mm) into a large skillet and heat over medium-high heat until the oil is very hot. Line a large plate with paper towels and set it near the stovetop. Working in batches if needed to avoid crowding, add the chicken to the hot oil and fry, turning once or twice, until the crust is crisp and deep golden brown and the chicken is cooked through, 7 to 9 minutes total. (The timing depends on the size and thickness of the pieces.) Using tongs or a slotted spoon, transfer to the towel-lined plate to drain. Repeat until all the chicken is cooked.

To serve, transfer the chicken to a serving platter and serve right away, with the ranch dressing alongside for dipping.

> Nutrition Values (per serving): Energy (kJ) ~1757 kJ, Calories ~420 kcal, Fat ~18 g, Saturated Fat ~3 g, Carbohydrate ~28 g, Sugar ~1 g, Dietary Fiber ~1 g, Protein ~32 g, Cholesterol ~115 mg, Sodium ~950 mg

Pasta Amatriciana

Amatriciana is a classic Italian pasta sauce that traditionally includes guanciale (cured pork cheek), tomatoes, pecorino cheese, black pepper, olive oil, and sometimes white wine. In this more elaborate version, smoky bacon and cremini mushrooms deepen the overall flavor and crushed and diced tomatoes, red wine, and a touch of balsamic vinegar create a heartier profile. Finished with a large splash of cream, the sauce is spooned atop freshly cooked pasta and then garnished with shaved Parmesan. Want a bit of spice? Add red pepper flakes to the sauce with the tomatoes.

MAKES 4 TO 6 SERVINGS

- 3 slices thick-cut bacon, cut crosswise into ½-inch (12-mm) pieces
- ½ yellow onion, thinly sliced
- Kosher salt and freshly ground pepper
- 1 Tbsp balsamic vinegar
- 8 oz (225 g) cremini mushrooms, stem ends trimmed and sliced
- ¼ cup (60 ml) dry red wine
- 1 (15-oz/430-g) can crushed tomatoes
- 1 (14.5-oz/415-g) can diced tomatoes, with juices
- ¼ cup (60 ml) water
- 2 Tbsp chopped fresh flat-leaf parsley, oregano, and/or basil
- ¼ cup (60 ml) heavy cream
- 1 lb (450 g) rigatoni or other short pasta shape
- Shaved Parmesan or ricotta salata cheese, for serving

To make the sauce, in a medium saucepan over medium-low heat, cook the bacon, stirring occasionally, until crisp, about 5 minutes. Using a slotted spoon, transfer to paper towels to drain and set aside.

Pour off all but 1 Tbsp of the bacon fat from the pan and return the pan to medium-low heat. Add the onion and a pinch of salt and cook, stirring, until the onion is tender and caramelized, 10 to 15 minutes.

Add the vinegar and stir to mix, then continue to simmer for about 1 minute. Add the mushrooms, season with salt, and cook, stirring occasionally, until they start to become tender, about 3 minutes. Add the wine, increase the heat to medium, and let simmer, stirring occasionally, for 2 minutes.

Add the crushed and diced tomatoes and juices and the water and season with salt and pepper. Bring to a simmer, then turn down the heat to low and simmer until the flavors come together, about 20 minutes. Stir in the reserved bacon and the herbs and then stir in the cream. Continue to simmer gently until heated through.

To cook the pasta, while the sauce is simmering, fill a large pot three-fourths full with salted water and bring to a boil over high heat. Add the pasta, bring the water back to a boil, and cook, stirring occasionally, until al dente, about 12 minutes or according to package directions. Drain into a colander.

To serve, divide the pasta evenly among four shallow bowls. Top each portion with plenty of the sauce and garnish with the Parmesan.

Nutrition Values (per serving for 6 servings): Energy (kJ) ~2175 kJ, Calories ~520 kcal, Fat ~20 g, Saturated Fat ~9 g, Carbohydrate ~58 g, Sugar ~8 g, Dietary Fiber ~4 g, Protein ~18 g, Cholesterol ~55 mg, Sodium ~680 mg

Tex-Mex Chicken Stew

This Tex-Mex stew is cozy, hearty, and full of bold, layered flavors. Chicken, black beans, fire-roasted tomatoes, and green chiles simmer in a richly spiced broth that's brightened with fresh lime juice. Serve the stew on its own, over steamed rice, or with warm tortillas. Don't skimp on the toppings. Cheese, avocado, cilantro, and tortilla chips deliver both flavor and texture.

MAKES 4 TO 6 SERVINGS

1 Tbsp vegetable oil

½ yellow onion, finely chopped

Kosher salt

2 Tbsp chili powder

2 tsp ground cumin

2 (14.5-oz/415-g) cans diced fire-roasted tomatoes, with juices

1 (15-oz/430-g) can black beans, drained and rinsed

2 (4-oz/115-g) cans diced mild green chiles, drained

Juice of 1 lime, plus lime wedges for serving

2½ cups (590 ml) chicken broth

2 cups (285 g) chopped or shredded cooked chicken (page 38)

½ cup (65 g) fresh or frozen corn kernels

¼ cup (10 g) finely chopped fresh cilantro, plus more for garnish

Shredded Monterey Jack or Cheddar cheese, for serving

1 large ripe avocado, halved, pitted, peeled, and thinly sliced or cubed, for serving

Tortilla chips, for serving

To make the stew, in a saucepan over medium heat, warm the oil. Add the onion and a pinch of salt and cook, stirring, until softened. Stir in the chili powder and cumin, then stir in the tomatoes, beans, chiles, lime juice, and 1 tsp salt. Bring to a simmer, cover partially, and simmer for 10 minutes to blend the flavors.

Add the broth and bring to a gentle boil, then turn down the heat to low and continue to simmer until the flavors come together, about 10 minutes. Add the chicken, cilantro, and corn and simmer gently until the chicken is warmed through and the corn is just cooked, about 5 minutes.

To serve, divide the stew evenly among four to six bowls. Top each serving with cheese, avocado, a handful of chips, and a sprinkle of cilantro and serve right away. Pass the lime wedges alongside.

Nutrition Values (per serving for 6 servings): Energy (kJ) ~1506 kJ, Calories ~360 kcal, Fat ~12 g, Saturated Fat ~3 g, Carbohydrate ~32 g, Sugar ~6 g, Dietary Fiber ~8 g, Protein ~28 g, Cholesterol ~65 mg, Sodium ~1,150 mg

Chicken Karaage

Marina Schulze from our Culinary Team grew up in a Japanese American community in California where chicken karaage was a potluck favorite. Brining adds flavor through and through before the chicken is double fried to perfection. It's an instant crowd-pleaser. Marina first made it at a Japanese restaurant in New York City, calling her mother for the recipe to create this signature dish.

MAKES 4 TO 6 SERVINGS

½ cup (120 ml) cooking sake

¼ cup (60 ml) soy sauce

¼ cup (50 g) sugar

8 garlic cloves, minced

2 Tbsp peeled and minced fresh ginger

2 lb (900 g) boneless, skinless chicken thighs, cut into 2-inch (5-cm) pieces

1 cup (240 g) Kewpie mayonnaise

2 Tbsp sriracha sauce

1 lemon, cut into five wedges

Vegetable oil, for deep-frying

1¼ cups (225 g) potato starch

Kosher salt

To marinate the chicken, in a large bowl, whisk together the sake, soy sauce, sugar, garlic, and ginger until the sugar dissolves. Add the chicken and turn to coat evenly. Cover and marinate in the refrigerator for at least 1 hour or up to 8 hours.

To make the sauce, in a bowl, stir together the mayonnaise, sriracha, and the juice of 1 lemon wedge. Cover and refrigerate until serving.

To fry the chicken, pour oil to a depth of 2 inches (5 cm) into a large pot (do not fill the pot more than half full) and heat over medium-high heat to 360°F (180°C) on a deep-frying thermometer. Place a wire rack on a quarter sheet pan and line the rack with paper towels. Set the sheet pan near the stovetop.

Put the potato starch into a wide, shallow bowl. Have ready a large sheet pan. One at a time, remove the chicken pieces from the marinade, letting any excess drip off, then dredge in the potato starch, coating well and tapping off the excess. Set aside on the sheet pan.

When the oil is ready, working in batches to avoid crowding, add the chicken to the hot oil and fry, turning once or twice with tongs, until golden on all sides, about 2 minutes (it will not be fully cooked). Using the tongs, transfer the chicken to the towel-lined rack and let rest for 1 minute. Let the oil return to temperature before adding the next batch.

Return the chicken to the hot oil for a second time and fry, turning, until crisp and cooked through, about 3 minutes. Transfer to the rack and season with salt.

To serve, transfer the chicken to a serving platter and serve hot with the spicy mayo and lemon wedges alongside.

Nutrition Values (per serving for 6 servings): Energy (kJ) ~3850 kJ, Calories ~920 kcal, Fat ~64 g, Saturated Fat ~12 g, Carbohydrate ~43 g, Sugar ~14 g, Dietary Fiber ~1 g, Protein ~46 g, Cholesterol ~255 mg, Sodium ~1420 mg

Curried Coconut Chicken & Broccoli Noodles

Inspired by khow suey, a South Asian noodle soup, this dish blends chicken, broccoli, and fresh noodles in a rich, creamy coconut-curry sauce. Aromatic spices, ginger, and garlic deepen the flavor, while lime and cilantro add a touch of brightness. This noodle bowl is easy to customize with your favorite noodles or vegetables.

MAKES 4 TO 6 SERVINGS

1 medium yellow onion, halved, then half chopped and half thinly sliced

2 Tbsp peeled and chopped fresh ginger

2 garlic cloves, chopped

1½ cups (360 ml) chicken broth, plus more if needed

1 Tbsp vegetable oil

Kosher salt and freshly ground black pepper

3 Tbsp all-purpose flour

1 tsp ground turmeric

1 Tbsp sweet paprika

½ tsp cayenne pepper (optional)

1 (13.5–fl oz/405-ml) can coconut milk, well shaken

Finely grated zest and juice of 1 lime, plus lime wedges for serving

2 cups (200 g) small broccoli florets

2 to 3 cups (285 to 430 g) shredded or chopped cooked chicken (page 38)

¼ cup (10 g) chopped fresh cilantro, plus more for garnish

1 lb (450 g) fresh Chinese wheat noodles, or 8 oz (225 g) dried spaghetti

To make the sauce, in a blender, combine the chopped onion half, ginger, garlic, and 1 cup (240 ml) of the broth and blend until smooth.

In a saucepan over medium heat, warm the oil. Add the sliced onion and a pinch of salt and cook, stirring, until golden brown, about 7 minutes.

Turn down the heat to medium-low and stir in the flour until fully incorporated with the onion. Then stir in the turmeric, paprika, and cayenne (if using), mixing well. Slowly pour in the remaining ½ cup (120 ml) broth while stirring constantly, then add the reserved onion puree, ½ tsp salt, and several grinds of black pepper and whisk until smooth. Bring to a simmer and cook, stirring constantly, for 2 minutes.

To finish the curry, stir in the coconut milk and lime zest and juice and continue to simmer, stirring often, for 5 minutes to blend the flavors. Add the broccoli and cook, stirring occasionally, until the broccoli is tender-crisp, about 5 minutes. Add the chicken and simmer until the chicken is warmed through, about 2 minutes. Stir in the cilantro. If the sauce is too thick for your liking, add a little more broth. Taste and adjust the seasoning with salt and black pepper if needed.

While the sauce is simmering, cook the noodles. Fill a large pot three-fourths full with salted water and bring to a boil over high heat. Add the noodles and cook, stirring occasionally, until al dente, according to package directions. Drain into a colander.

To serve, divide the noodles among four to six bowls, then ladle the curry over the noodles, dividing it evenly. Garnish with cilantro and the lime wedges and serve at once.

Nutrition Values (per serving for 6 servings): Energy (kJ) ~2010 kJ, Calories ~480 kcal, Fat ~22 g, Saturated Fat ~14 g, Carbohydrate ~45 g, Sugar ~6 g, Dietary Fiber ~4 g, Protein ~28 g, Cholesterol ~65 mg, Sodium ~720 mg

7 Plant-Powered Plates

"Every garden holds a thousand meals waiting to be imagined."

–Avram Salzmann, HelloFresh Test Kitchen

There's a reason plant-powered eating has moved from trendy to a timeless practice. It makes us feel good. Study after study shows what many of us have sensed intuitively for years: that meals built around vegetables, fruits, legumes, and whole grains can have a profound impact on our long-term health.

Diets rich in plant-based foods are associated with lower risks of heart disease, type 2 diabetes, and certain cancers, and even a modest shift toward plants can improve energy levels, digestion, and overall well-being. One study found that replacing just one daily serving of red meat with beans or lentils can reduce chronic disease risk by up to 14 percent. That's the power of plants: small changes, big impact.

But beyond the health benefits, there's a practical truth that home cooks often discover with delight: Plant-based cooking is refreshingly simple. Vegetables and legumes don't require long cooking times or intricate techniques. A can of black beans becomes dinner in minutes. Cauliflower transforms with a quick roast. A handful of fresh herbs can wake up an entire dish. And because plants come naturally packed with color, texture, and flavor, your plate starts to look beautiful before you've done much at all.

This chapter celebrates the kind of meals that leave you feeling nourished, energized, and proud of what you've put on the table. The recipes are vibrant, approachable, and deeply satisfying, proof that cooking with plants is about abundance, not limitations. Our hope is that these dishes will bring ease, curiosity, and a little extra vitality to your everyday cooking—one plant-powered plate at a time.

Cheese Tortelloni with Mushroom Sauce

Umami—the elusive "fifth taste"—is what makes this dish impossible to resist. Delicate cheese-filled tortelloni are coated in a creamy, earthy mushroom sauce and finished with scallion greens for crunch and a pinch of red pepper flakes for subtle heat. Savory, comforting, and full of depth, this recipe delivers big flavor in no time, making it the kind of dish that has everyone reaching for seconds almost before the cook can even sit down.

MAKES 4 SERVINGS

Olive oil, for drizzling

1 lb (450 g) small button mushrooms, stem ends trimmed and quartered

1 (18-oz/505-g) package fresh cheese tortelloni

4 scallions, white and green parts, thinly sliced and parts kept separate

4 garlic cloves, minced

2 Tbsp Italian seasoning

4 Tbsp (55 g) unsalted butter

Kosher salt and freshly ground black pepper

4 Tbsp (60 g) cream cheese, cut into cubes

¼ cup (60 g) sour cream

2 Tbsp mushroom broth concentrate

Grated Parmesan cheese, for serving

Red pepper flakes, for serving

To make the mushrooms, in a large skillet over medium-high heat, warm a generous drizzle of oil. Add the mushrooms and cook, stirring occasionally, until softened and browned, 7 to 9 minutes.

To cook the tortelloni, while the mushrooms cook, fill a large pot three-fourths full with salted water and bring to a boil over high heat. Turn down the heat to medium-low, add the tortelloni, and simmer, stirring occasionally, until the tortelloni are tender and floating on the surface, 3 to 5 minutes. Scoop out ⅓ cup (80 ml) of the pasta water and reserve for the sauce. Drain the tortelloni and set aside.

To make the sauce, add the scallion whites, garlic, 1 Tbsp of the Italian seasoning, and 2 Tbsp of the butter to the skillet with the mushrooms and cook over medium-high heat, stirring, until the scallion whites have softened and the butter has melted, 1 to 2 minutes. Season with salt and black pepper. Turn down the heat to low and add the cream cheese, sour cream, mushroom broth concentrate, the ⅓ cup (80 ml) pasta water, and the remaining 2 Tbsp butter. Stir until the cream cheese and butter have melted and the mixture is thoroughly blended and warmed through.

To assemble, using a slotted spoon, transfer the tortelloni to the skillet and stir gently to coat evenly. If needed, stir in more pasta water, a little at a time, until the pasta is coated in the creamy sauce. Season with the remaining 1 Tbsp Italian seasoning and with salt and black pepper.

To serve, divide the pasta evenly among four shallow bowls. Sprinkle with Parmesan, the scallion greens, and red pepper flakes and serve.

Nutrition Values (per serving): Energy (kJ) 3222 kJ, Calories 770 kcal, Fat 46 g, Saturated Fat 26 g, Carbohydrate 57 g, Sugar 7 g, Dietary Fiber 6 g, Protein 27 g, Cholesterol 145 mg, Sodium 1150 mg

Chiles Rellenos with Creamy Corn

These chile rellenos are a light and simple take on the classic, forgoing the fluffy fried egg batter for roasted chiles. The mildly spicy chiles are paired with a creamy corn filling and fresh tomato salsa that are superb when made with sweet summer corn and ripe tomatoes.

MAKES 4 SERVINGS

CHILE RELLENOS

4 large poblano chiles

2 Tbsp unsalted butter

½ cup (70 g) finely chopped white onion

Kosher salt and freshly ground pepper

1 large garlic clove, minced

1½ Tbsp all-purpose flour

½ cup (120 ml) whole milk, plus more if needed

3 cups (390 g) fresh or frozen white corn kernels

¾ cup (85 g) shredded Oaxaca or low-moisture mozzarella cheese

2 Tbsp fresh lime juice

¼ cup (10 g) chopped fresh cilantro

FRESH TOMATO SALSA

2 large ripe but slightly firm heirloom tomatoes, halved, seeded, and chopped (about 2 cups/320 g)

¼ cup (35 g) finely chopped white onion

2 Tbsp chopped fresh cilantro

2 Tbsp fresh lime juice

Kosher salt

1 lime, quartered

Warmed corn tortillas, for serving

Roast the chiles over the flame of a gas stove on high heat, turning often with tongs, until the chiles are blackened all over and the skin is blistered. Transfer the chiles to a bowl and cover with a plate to steam until cool enough to handle, about 20 minutes. (Alternatively, broil the chiles in the oven until blackened.)

Using your hands or paper towels, rub off and discard the blackened skin from each chile. Cut each chile lengthwise from stem end to blossom end, being careful not to cut the chile in half. Cut out and discard the core, seeds, and inner membranes. Set the chiles aside.

To make the salsa, in a bowl, stir together the tomatoes, onion, cilantro, and lime juice. Season with salt and stir gently to combine. Taste and adjust with more lime juice if needed. Set aside.

To make the corn filling, in a skillet over medium heat, melt the butter. Add the onion and a pinch of salt and cook, stirring, until the onion has softened, about 4 minutes. Add the garlic and cook, stirring, until fragrant, about 1 minute. Turn down the heat to medium-low and stir in the flour. Slowly pour in the milk while stirring constantly, then continue to stir until the mixture thickens. Let the mixture bubble, stirring, for 1 minute. Add the corn and cook, stirring, until the corn is tender-crisp, about 3 minutes. Stir in the cheese until melted. If the sauce is too thick, add a splash more milk. Stir in the lime juice. Taste and adjust the seasoning with salt, pepper, and lime juice if needed. Stir in the cilantro. Remove from the heat and cover to keep warm.

To assemble and serve, arrange the roasted chiles on a microwave-safe plate and rewarm in the microwave. For each serving, place a chile on a plate and open it up like a book. Spoon one-fourth of the corn mixture into the center and spoon some of the salsa over the top. Serve the chiles warm with the lime wedges and tortillas alongside.

Nutrition Values (per serving): Energy (kJ) ~1760 kJ, Calories ~420 kcal, Fat ~22 g, Saturated Fat ~11 g, Carbohydrate ~42 g, Sugar ~8 g, Dietary Fiber ~6 g, Protein ~14 g, Cholesterol ~45 mg, Sodium ~680 mg

Gochujang Mushroom Quesadillas with Napa Slaw

Gochujang, a Korean fermented chile paste, brings a sweet, spicy, and umami-rich punch to these quesadillas, creating a playful mash-up of Korean and Mexican flavors. Mushrooms are quickly cooked, tossed with gochujang, and then sandwiched along with melty cheese between flour tortillas. An Asian-inspired cabbage slaw tops each quesadilla just before serving.

MAKES 4 SERVINGS

SLAW

1 Tbsp gochujang

1 Tbsp rice vinegar

1 Tbsp vegetable oil

½ tsp Asian fish sauce

½ tsp sugar

¼ tsp toasted sesame oil

Pinch of kosher salt

3 cups (85 g) shredded napa cabbage (about 6 oz)

2 scallions, white and green parts, thinly sliced

2 Tbsp chopped fresh cilantro

QUESADILLAS

Vegetable oil, for cooking

1¼ lb (570 g) cremini or button mushrooms, stem ends trimmed and sliced

Kosher salt

1 Tbsp gochujang

8 (8-inch/20-cm) flour tortillas

2 cups (240g) shredded Monterey Jack or low-moisture mozzarella cheese

To make the slaw, in a medium bowl, whisk together the gochujang, vinegar, vegetable oil, fish sauce, sugar, sesame oil, and salt, mixing well. Add the cabbage, scallions, and cilantro and toss to coat evenly. Cover and refrigerate until ready to use. (The slaw can be made up to 1 hour in advance.)

To cook the mushrooms, in a large skillet (preferably nonstick) over medium heat, warm a drizzle of vegetable oil. Add the mushrooms and a big pinch of salt and cook, stirring occasionally, until the mushrooms release their liquid, the liquid cooks off, and the mushrooms brown, about 4 minutes. (If liquid remains, pour it off.) Transfer the mushrooms to a bowl and stir in the gochujang. Wipe out the skillet and reserve.

To assemble the quesadillas, line up four of the tortillas on a work surface. Top with half of the cheese, dividing it evenly and spreading it in a thin layer. Add one-fourth of the mushrooms to each cheese-topped tortilla, arranging the mushrooms in an even layer. Top with the remaining cheese, dividing it evenly and spreading it an even layer. Top the layered tortillas with the remaining four tortillas.

To cook the quesadillas, warm the reserved skillet over medium heat. Brush lightly with vegetable oil. Add one filled quesadilla to the pan and cook until the bottom is golden brown, about 2 minutes. Flip and cook the other side until golden brown and the cheese is melted, about 2 minutes longer. Transfer to a plate. Repeat with the remaining quesadillas.

To serve, top each quesadilla with one-fourth of the slaw and serve.

Nutrition Values (per serving): Energy (kJ) ~2175 kJ, Calories ~520 kcal, Fat ~24 g, Saturated Fat ~10 g, Carbohydrate ~52 g, Sugar ~6 g, Dietary Fiber ~4 g, Protein ~20 g, Cholesterol ~40 mg, Sodium ~620 mg

Roasted Cauliflower Tikka Masala

This plant-based take on the much-loved chicken tikka masala swaps tender cauliflower for the usual protein while keeping all the rich, warming spices that make the original so popular. Roasting the florets deepens their flavor, and a creamy spiced coconut milk–tomato sauce cloaks them with richness. Finished with fresh cilantro and a squeeze of lemon, this vegan riff on the British–South Asian classic can be served over steamed rice or with warm naan.

MAKES 4 SERVINGS

- 2 tsp garam masala
- 1 tsp ground turmeric
- 1 tsp ground cumin
- 1 tsp sweet paprika
- ½ tsp ground ginger
- Kosher salt and freshly ground pepper
- 1 medium head cauliflower (about 2 lb/900 g), cored and cut into florets
- 4 Tbsp (60 ml) vegetable oil
- ½ yellow onion, finely chopped
- 2 garlic cloves, minced
- 2 Tbsp tomato paste
- 1 (14½-oz/415-g) can crushed tomatoes
- ¼ cup (60 ml) water
- 1 cup (240 ml) well-shaken canned coconut milk or coconut cream
- 1 Tbsp fresh lemon juice, plus more if needed
- ¼ cup (10 g) chopped fresh cilantro, plus more for garnish
- Steamed rice and/or warmed naan, for serving

To roast the cauliflower, preheat the oven to 450°F (230°C). In a bowl, stir together the garam masala, turmeric, cumin, paprika, ginger, and 1 tsp salt.

Put the cauliflower on a large sheet pan, drizzle with 2 Tbsp of the oil, and toss until evenly coated. Add 1 Tbsp of the spice mixture and a few grinds of pepper and toss until evenly coated. Spread the cauliflower in an even layer. Roast, turning once or twice, until golden and tender-crisp, 12 to 15 minutes.

To make the sauce, while the cauliflower roasts, in a large saucepan over medium heat, warm the remaining 2 Tbsp oil. Add the onion and cook, stirring occasionally, until tender, about 5 minutes. Turn down the heat to medium-low and stir in the garlic, then add the tomato paste and the remaining spice mixture. Cook, stirring, until fragrant, about 1 minute.

Add the tomatoes and water and stir to combine, scraping up any browned bits from the pan bottom. Bring to a gentle boil, then turn down the heat to low and simmer, stirring occasionally, until the sauce thickens slightly, about 4 minutes.

To finish the curry, uncover, add the roasted cauliflower, coconut milk, and lemon juice, and stir well. Bring to a simmer, re-cover, and cook, stirring occasionally, until the cauliflower is done to your liking, about 10 minutes for tender. If the sauce becomes too thick for your liking, add more coconut milk or water. Taste and adjust the seasoning with more lemon juice if needed. Stir in the cilantro. Spoon the curry over rice and garnish with more cilantro, then serve at once.

Nutrition Values (per serving): Energy (kJ) ~1510 kJ, Calories ~360 kcal, Fat ~24 g, Saturated Fat ~14 g, Carbohydrate ~28 g, Sugar ~8 g, Dietary Fiber ~7 g, Protein ~6 g, Cholesterol ~0 mg, Sodium ~620 mg

Mushroom Bahn Mi

Banh mì, the iconic Vietnamese sandwich, is celebrated for its layers of savory, pickled, and fresh flavors, and this mushroom version from our brand partner Roland Foods brings a plant-based twist. Packed with umami from mushrooms, miso, and vegan oyster sauce, it is a perfect balance of earthy, tangy, and slightly spicy. Inspired by Roland Foods' heritage—the first product they brought to market over ninety years ago was premium dried mushrooms from France—this globally influenced sandwich highlights Southeast Asian flavors with plant-forward innovation.

MAKES 4 SANDWICHES

CARROT DAIKON SLAW

1 cup (240 ml) water

2 tsp kosher salt

1 Tbsp sugar

1 cup (240 ml) rice vinegar

1 small daikon radish, peeled and cut into matchsticks (about 2 cups/220 g)

1 large carrot, peeled and cut into matchsticks (about 2 cups/220 g)

MUSHROOM PÂTÉ

1 cup (45 g) dried shiitake mushrooms

1 cup (240 ml) boiling water

1 Tbsp toasted sesame oil

1 large shallot, minced

1 cup (60 g) sliced fresh cremini mushrooms

2 Tbsp white miso

4 Tbsp (55 g) unsalted butter, cut into Tbsp-size cubes

To make the slaw, in a small saucepan over high heat, bring ½ cup (120 ml) of the water to a boil. Add the salt and sugar and stir until completely dissolved. Remove the pan from the heat, add the remaining ½ cup (120 ml) water and the vinegar, and stir to combine. Add the daikon and carrot to the brine and set aside for 20 minutes. Use right away or transfer to an airtight container and refrigerate for up to 1 month.

To make the mushroom pâté, in a medium heatproof bowl, combine the shiitake mushrooms and the boiling water and set aside for about 30 minutes until rehydrated and plump. Remove the mushrooms from the water and cut off and discard the tough stems. Reserve the soaking water.

While the shiitakes soak, in a large skillet over medium-high heat, warm the sesame oil. Add the shallot and cremini mushrooms and cook, stirring, until the mushrooms soften and brown and the liquid evaporates, about 10 minutes. Remove from the heat and transfer to a food processor. Wipe out the skillet and reserve.

Add the rehydrated shiitake mushrooms, 1 Tbsp of the soaking water, and the miso to the processor and process, stopping to scrape down the sides of the bowl as needed, until a smooth paste forms. With the motor running, add the butter, 1 Tbsp at a time, processing until fully incorporated. You should have about 1¼ cups (300 g) pâté.

continued . . .

"Somewhere a carrot is finally getting the credit it deserves."

–Michelle

Mushroom Bahn Mi

continued from page 208 . . .

To cook the oyster mushrooms, in a small bowl, stir together the hoisin sauce, oyster sauce, and chile oil, mixing well. Return the large skillet to medium heat and warm the grapeseed oil. Add the oyster mushrooms and cook, stirring occasionally, until caramelized on both sides and their liquid has evaporated, about 8 minutes. (Cook the mushrooms in two batches if they are too crowded in the pan, as they won't caramelize properly.) Remove from the heat and stir in the hoisin mixture. Taste and season with salt if needed.

To assemble the sandwiches, split each baguette piece horizontally and arrange the halves cut-side up on a work surface. Scoop the pâté onto the cut side of each baguette piece, dividing it evenly and spreading it in an even layer. Top the bottom half of each sandwich with one-fourth of the oyster mushroom mixture, then add the slaw, dividing it evenly. Finally, top the slaw with the cilantro sprigs, chile slices, and radish slices, close with the baguette tops, and serve.

OYSTER MUSHROOMS

1 Tbsp hoisin sauce

1 Tbsp vegan oyster sauce, preferably Roland

1 tsp chile oil

1 Tbsp grapeseed or vegetable oil

1 lb (450 g) fresh oyster mushrooms, torn into bite-size pieces

Kosher salt

1 baguette, cut crosswise into four equal lengths, or 4 crusty rolls

Fresh cilantro sprigs, for garnish

1 jalapeño, serrano, or Fresno chile, thinly sliced

2 to 3 radishes, thinly sliced

Nutrition Values (per sandwich): Energy (kJ) ~2010 kJ, Calories ~480 kcal, Fat ~22 g, Saturated Fat ~8 g, Carbohydrate ~52 g, Sugar ~8 g, Dietary Fiber ~5 g, Protein ~12 g, Cholesterol ~20 mg, Sodium ~1,000 mg

Tofu Herb Lettuce Wraps

Inspired by the bright, herb-packed flavors of Southeast Asian larb—the popular minced meat salad typically made with pork or chicken—this plant-forward variation leans on tofu to soak up all the zesty goodness. Pressing, finely chopping, and then searing the tofu without stirring helps it brown and crisp and soak up the punchy mix of lime, fish sauce (or coconut aminos), scallions, garlic, and fresh herbs. Spoon the mixture into cool lettuce leaves, add peanuts for crunch, and you've got a new, vibrant take on larb that rivals the original.

MAKES 8 LETTUCE WRAPS; 4 SERVINGS

- 1 (14- to 16-oz/400- to 450-g) block firm tofu, drained and halved crosswise
- 1 Tbsp vegetable oil
- 1 shallot, minced
- 2 scallions, white and green parts, thinly sliced and parts kept separate
- 2 garlic cloves, minced
- 1 small fresh Thai chile, minced (optional)
- 2 Tbsp fresh lime juice
- 2 tsp Asian fish sauce or coconut aminos
- 1 tsp soy sauce
- 1½ tsp packed light brown sugar
- 1 small Persian cucumber, finely diced
- 2 Tbsp finely chopped fresh cilantro, plus chopped for garnish
- 2 Tbsp finely chopped fresh mint leaves, plus chopped for garnish
- Kosher salt and freshly ground pepper
- 8 small iceberg or butter lettuce leaves, for serving
- Chopped salted roasted peanuts, for serving
- 4 lime wedges, for serving

To press the tofu, pat the tofu blocks dry with paper towels, then wrap them tightly in a kitchen towel and place on a small sheet pan. Place a heavy weight, such as a cast-iron skillet, on top of the tofu to weigh it down. Set aside at room temperature for 30 minutes.

To shred the tofu, unwrap the two blocks and shred them on the large holes of a box grater-shredder onto a cutting board. Then, using a large, sharp knife, roughly chop the shredded tofu.

To make the tofu filling, in a large skillet over medium heat, warm the oil. Add the shallot, scallion whites, garlic, and Thai chile (if using) and cook, stirring frequently, until fragrant, about 30 seconds. Add the tofu and stir to mix well. Cook without stirring for 2 minutes, then stir. Continue to cook, stirring every so often, until the tofu is golden brown, about 5 minutes longer.

While the tofu browns, in a small bowl, whisk together the lime juice, fish sauce, soy sauce, and brown sugar until the sugar dissolves. When the tofu is ready, add the lime juice mixture to the skillet, stir to combine, and remove from the heat. Transfer to a medium bowl and let cool to room temperature. Taste and adjust the seasoning with soy sauce, fish sauce, and lime juice to your liking.

Add the cucumber and finely chopped cilantro and mint to the tofu mixture and stir until well mixed. Season with salt and pepper.

To assemble and serve, spoon the tofu mixture into the lettuce leaves, dividing it evenly. Garnish with the cilantro, mint, scallion greens, and peanuts and serve, with the lime wedges alongside.

Nutrition Values (per 2-wrap serving): Energy (kJ) ~1090 kJ, Calories ~260 kcal, Fat ~14 g, Saturated Fat ~2 g, Carbohydrate ~16 g, Sugar ~6 g, Dietary Fiber ~4 g, Protein ~14 g, Cholesterol ~0 mg, Sodium ~550 mg

Poblano Chile & Black Bean Enchiladas

These enchiladas lean delightfully Tex-Mex, offering all the saucy satisfaction without sticking to tradition. Soft flour tortillas are wrapped around a hearty mix of roasted poblano chiles, black beans, and tomatoes, then generously covered in bright salsa verde and melty Jack cheese.

MAKES 4 SERVINGS

Vegetable oil, for drizzling

2 poblano chiles, seeded and diced

2 Roma tomatoes, finely diced

4 scallions, white and green parts, thinly sliced and parts kept separate

1 (15-oz/430-g) can black beans, drained with liquid reserved separately

2 Tbsp Southwest spice blend or chili powder

Kosher salt and freshly ground pepper

2 Tbsp unsalted butter

12 (8-inch/20-cm) flour tortillas, warmed

1 (14-oz/400-g) container green salsa, warmed

½ cup (60 g) shredded Monterey Jack cheese

¼ cup (60 g) sour cream

1 or 2 small fresh red chiles, thinly sliced (optional)

Position an oven rack in the upper third of the oven and preheat the oven to 475°F (245°F).

To make the filling, in a large skillet over medium-high heat, warm a drizzle of oil. Add the poblano chiles and cook, stirring, just until softened, 3 to 4 minutes. Add the tomatoes, scallion whites, half of the beans, 2 Tbsp of the reserved bean liquid, and all but 1 tsp of the Southwest spice blend, and cook, stirring, until warmed through, 2 to 3 minutes. Season with salt and pepper. Remove from the heat.

To make the mashed beans, in a small pot over medium-high heat, warm a generous drizzle of oil. Add the remaining beans and cook, stirring, until slightly softened, 2 to 3 minutes. Add ⅓ cup (80 ml) of the reserved bean liquid and simmer until warmed through, 1 to 2 minutes. Turn down the heat to low and stir in the butter until melted. Turn off the heat. Using a potato masher or fork, mash the beans until mostly smooth. Season with plenty of salt and pepper.

To assemble the enchiladas, have ready a 9-by-13-inch (23-by-33-cm) baking dish. Line up the tortillas on a work surface. Spread the top of each tortilla with the mashed bean mixture, dividing it evenly. Spoon the filling onto one half of each tortilla, dividing it evenly. Starting from the edge with the filling, roll up each tortilla then arrange them, seam-side down, in the baking dish. Spoon the salsa over the top, then sprinkle with the cheese. Bake until bubbly and the cheese melts, 3 to 5 minutes.

Meanwhile, add the sour cream to a bowl with the 1 tsp Southwest spice blend and stir to mix. Add warm water, 1 tsp at a time, until the mixture has a drizzling consistency. Season with salt and pepper.

To serve, drizzle the enchiladas with the sour cream mixture, then sprinkle with the scallion greens and chile slices (if using) and serve.

Nutrition Values (per serving): Energy (kJ) ~3070kJ, Calories ~735 kcal, Fat ~27 g, Saturated Fat ~11 g, Carbohydrate ~99 g, Sugar ~8 g, Dietary Fiber ~11 g, Protein ~24 g, Cholesterol ~28 mg, Sodium ~900mg

Black Bean Tostadas with Kale Slaw

These black bean tostadas are full of flavor and texture. Purchased corn tostadas and canned beans speed up prep time. Spiced beans and a crunchy, tangy slaw of cabbage, kale, carrot, pickled onion, and lime layered with Cotija cheese and avocado makes the perfect topping.

MAKES 4 SERVINGS

SLAW

2 cups (100 g) finely shredded red or green cabbage, or a mixture

1 cup (60 g) stemmed and finely shredded dinosaur kale leaves

1 medium carrot, finely shredded

¼ cup (30 g) chopped pickled onions (page 79), plus more for garnish

2 Tbsp chopped fresh cilantro, plus more for garnish

Juice of ½ lime, plus 8 thin wedges for garnish

2 tsp vegetable oil

Kosher salt and freshly ground pepper

TOSTADAS

Vegetable oil, for cooking

¼ cup (35 g) chopped onion

1 large garlic clove, minced

Kosher salt and freshly ground pepper

1 tsp ground cumin

2 (15-oz/430-g) cans black beans, drained and rinsed

½ cup (120 ml) vegetable or chicken broth

8 (5-inch/13-cm) corn tostadas,

½ cup (60 g) crumbled Cotija cheese, queso fresco, or feta

1 large ripe avocado, halved, pitted, peeled, and sliced

To make the slaw, in a bowl, combine the cabbage, kale, carrot, pickled onions, and cilantro. Drizzle with the lime juice and oil and season with salt and pepper. Toss to coat evenly. Taste and adjust with more lime juice if needed. (The slaw can be made up to 2 hours in advance and refrigerated in an airtight container.)

To make the beans, in a saucepan over medium-low heat, warm a drizzle of oil. Add the onion, garlic, and a pinch of salt and cook, stirring occasionally, until the onion softens, about 3 minutes. Stir in the cumin, then add the beans and broth. Season with salt and pepper and stir to mix well. Increase the heat to medium-high and bring to a boil. Turn down the heat to low, cover partially, and simmer, stirring occasionally, for 10 minutes to heat through and blend the flavors. Using a fork, partially smash the beans. They should be thickened without much liquid but spreadable. If they seem too dry, add a splash of water.

To assemble and serve, warm the tostadas according to package directions. Place two tostadas on each plate. Divide the beans evenly among the tostadas, gently spreading them into an even layer. Top each serving with the cheese, followed by a mound of the slaw, and then the avocado, dividing them evenly.

Garnish each tostada with cilantro, pickled onions, and a wedge of lime and serve.

Nutrition Values (per serving): Energy (kJ) ~1760 kJ, Calories ~420 kcal, Fat ~18 g, Saturated Fat ~4 g, Carbohydrate ~52 g, Sugar ~6 g, Dietary Fiber ~12 g, Protein ~14 g, Cholesterol ~10 mg, Sodium ~680 mg

Halloumi Greek Salad Wraps with Tzatziki

Halloumi, a firm, salty cheese from Cyprus, holds its shape when cooked, making it perfect for panfrying until golden and slightly crisp. Here, it's layered in a wrap with a bright Greek salad and creamy tzatziki. Flour tortillas make an easy wrap, but you can go with lavash instead or tuck everything into pita breads.

MAKES 4 WRAPS

GREEK SALAD

2 Persian cucumbers, quartered lengthwise and sliced

1 cup (170 g) quartered cherry tomatoes

¼ small red onion, thinly sliced

Extra virgin olive oil, for drizzling

2 tsp red wine vinegar

½ tsp dried oregano

Kosher salt and freshly ground pepper

TZATZIKI

½ Persian cucumber

1 small garlic clove

1 cup (240 g) plain Greek yogurt

2 tsp fresh lemon juice

2 tsp chopped fresh dill

4 (12-inch/30-cm) flour tortillas

Extra virgin olive oil, for drizzling

12 oz (340 g) halloumi cheese, cut into 16 wide slices

To make the salad, in a medium bowl, toss together the cucumbers, tomatoes, onion, a drizzle of oil, the vinegar, and oregano. Season with salt and pepper and set aside.

To make the tzatziki, shred the cucumber on the large holes of a box grater-shredder. Blot dry with paper towels and transfer to a small bowl. Grate the garlic on the small holes and add to the bowl. Add the yogurt, lemon juice, and dill and stir well.

To warm the tortillas, heat a large nonstick skillet over medium heat. Have ready a kitchen towel. One at a time, add the tortillas to the pan and heat, turning once, until pliable and dotted with light brown spots, about 30 seconds on each side. As each tortilla is ready, transfer it to the towel, stacking the tortillas as you go and wrapping them to keep them warm.

To sear the halloumi, with the skillet still over medium heat, drizzle in a little oil. When the oil is hot, add the halloumi slices and sear without turning until golden brown on the underside, about 1 minute. Turn and sear until the second side is golden brown and the cheese is hot throughout, 1 to 2 minutes.

To assemble and serve, line up the warm tortillas on a work surface. Divide the tzatziki evenly among the tortillas, spreading it on the lower half of each tortilla and leaving a 1-inch (2.5-cm) border. Mound the salad in the middle of the tzatziki, dividing it evenly, and then top each mound with four slices of the halloumi. Fold in the sides of each tortilla, then roll the tortilla up like a burrito. Serve at once.

Nutrition Values (per wrap): Energy (kJ) ~2175 kJ, Calories ~520 kcal, Fat ~28 g, Saturated Fat ~14 g, Carbohydrate ~40 g, Sugar ~6 g, Dietary Fiber ~3 g, Protein ~24 g, Cholesterol ~65 mg, Sodium ~1,000 mg

Pasta Parmesan with Peppers & Herbs

Here, an old-school classic, pasta in tomato sauce, becomes a full-on feast with just a few flavorful additions. This penne in marinara gets a boost from sweet bell peppers, fragrant herbs, a golden cheese-and-breadcrumb topping, and a drizzle of basil oil. Plus, this harmonious mix of tastes and textures is ready to serve within just minutes of putting the pasta water on to boil.

MAKES 4 SERVINGS

12 oz (340 g) penne

Olive oil, for drizzling

2 red bell peppers, seeded and diced

1 yellow onion, diced

4 garlic cloves, minced

2 Tbsp Tuscan heat spice or 1¾ Tbsp Italian seasoning blend mixed with ½ tsp garlic powder and ½ tsp red pepper flakes

Kosher salt and freshly ground black pepper

1 (24-oz/680-g) jar marinara sauce

½ cup (15 g) grated Parmesan cheese

½ cup (30 g) panko breadcrumbs

8 oz (225 g) fresh mozzarella cheese, cut into ½-inch (12-mm) cubes

Basil-infused olive oil, for serving

To cook the pasta, fill a large pot three-fourths full with salted water and bring to a boil over high heat. Add the penne, bring the water back to a boil, and cook, stirring occasionally, until al dente, about 9 minutes or according to package directions. Scoop out ¾ cup (180 ml) of the pasta water, then drain the pasta and set the reserved water and pasta aside separately.

Meanwhile, make the sauce. In a large ovenproof skillet over medium heat, warm a generous drizzle of olive oil. Add the bell peppers and cook, stirring, until tender, 4 to 6 minutes. Stir in the onion, garlic, and 1 Tbsp of the Tuscan heat spice and cook, stirring, until the onion has softened, 3 to 5 minutes. Season with salt and black pepper.

To assemble, add the marinara sauce, penne, the remaining 1 Tbsp Tuscan heat spice, and the ¾ cup (180 ml) pasta water to the skillet and stir to mix well. Simmer, stirring, until warmed through, 3 to 4 minutes. Stir in half of the Parmesan, then season with plenty of salt and black pepper.

While the pasta simmers, position an oven rack in the upper third of the oven and preheat the broiler.

To make the topping, in a bowl, stir together the panko, the remaining Parmesan, and a drizzle of olive oil. Top the pasta with the mozzarella in an even layer, then sprinkle evenly with the panko mixture.

Broil the pasta until the topping is golden brown, the sauce is bubbly, and the cheese has melted, 5 to 7 minutes.

To serve, divide among four plates. Drizzle with basil oil and serve.

Nutrition Values (per serving): Energy (kJ) 3473 kJ, Calories 830 kcal, Fat 40 g, Saturated Fat 13 g, Carbohydrate 93 g, Sugar 16 g, Dietary Fiber 7 g, Protein 27 g, Cholesterol 55 mg, Sodium 1010 mg

Smoky Lentil Sloppy Joes

Sloppy joes are classic comfort food—messy, saucy, and utterly satisfying—and this plant-based version is just as tempting. Green lentils hold their shape when cooked and give the filling a hearty texture, while smoked paprika, cumin, and sweet bell peppers add a pleasing mix of flavors. Spoon the lentils onto toasted buns or over roasted sweet potatoes and top with Cheddar (or vegan) cheese, then dig into a dish that delivers all the nostalgic goodness of the traditional sloppy joe.

MAKES 4 TO 6 SERVINGS

1 cup (200 g) green lentils

1 Tbsp vegetable oil

½ yellow onion, finely chopped

½ red bell pepper, seeded and finely chopped

½ green bell pepper, seeded and finely chopped

1 celery stalk, finely chopped

Kosher salt and freshly ground black pepper

1 cup (240 g) tomato sauce

¼ cup (65 g) ketchup

2 Tbsp country Dijon mustard

1 Tbsp packed light brown sugar, plus more if needed

1 Tbsp apple cider vinegar, plus more if needed

1 teaspoon chili powder

1 teaspoon ground cumin

½ teaspoon smoked paprika

Toasted burger buns or roasted sweet potatoes (page 54), for serving

Shredded Cheddar cheese, for serving

To cook the lentils, in a small saucepan over medium-high heat, bring 3 cups (720 ml) water to a boil. Add the lentils and stir to combine. Boil, stirring occasionally, until the lentils are tender but not mushy, about 20 minutes. Drain off any excess liquid and set aside.

Meanwhile, make the sauce. In a medium saucepan over medium heat, warm the oil. Add the onion, red and green bell peppers, celery, and a big pinch of salt and cook, stirring occasionally, until tender and starting to brown, about 7 minutes. Add the tomato sauce, ketchup, Dijon mustard, brown sugar, vinegar, chili powder, cumin, paprika, 1 tsp salt, and ½ tsp black pepper and bring to a simmer, stirring. Turn down the heat to medium-low, cover partially, and simmer, stirring frequently, until the flavors come together and the mixture is slightly thickened, about 5 minutes.

Add the lentils and stir to mix. Bring to a simmer, then turn down the heat to low, cover partially, and simmer, stirring occasionally, until the mixture comes together, about 5 minutes. You want the mixture to be quite thick. If it is too thick, adjust the consistency with a little water. Taste and adjust the seasoning with salt, pepper, sugar, and/or vinegar if needed.

To serve, pile the lentil mixture onto the toasted bun bottoms or sweet potatoes. Top with cheese and close with a bun top, if using. Serve at once.

Nutrition Values (per serving for 6 servings): Energy (kJ) ~1000 kJ, Calories ~240 kcal, Fat ~6 g, Saturated Fat ~1 g, Carbohydrate ~37 g, Sugar ~9 g, Dietary Fiber ~9 g, Protein ~10 g, Cholesterol ~0 mg, Sodium ~460 mg

Turkish Eggs with Yogurt & Herb Salad

A Turkish breakfast classic, this dish features poached eggs atop creamy garlic-infused yogurt—or labneh for a tangier twist—finished with a simple chile butter and a cucumber-herb salad. Aleppo pepper flakes lend a distinctive warmth and fruitiness to the butter, but you can substitute sweet paprika and a pinch of red pepper flakes for a different kind of heat. Served with warm pita for scooping, it's a welcome meal any hour of the day.

To make the herbed garlic yogurt, in a small bowl, stir together the yogurt, garlic, and dill. Season with salt and pepper. Set aside.

To make the smoky chile butter, in a small saucepan over medium-low heat, melt the butter. Add the Aleppo pepper flakes, paprika, cumin, and salt and simmer until fragrant, about 1 minute. Remove from heat and set aside.

To make the herb salad, in a bowl, toss together the cucumbers, lettuce, dill, and parsley. Drizzle with a little oil, add the lemon juice and salt, and toss to coat evenly. Set aside.

To poach the eggs, pour water to a depth of about 2 inches (5 cm) into a large, wide saucepan and bring to a boil over high heat. Turn down the heat to medium-low and stir in the vinegar. Have ready a small plate lined with a paper towel and a large plate for the cooked eggs. Crack an egg into a small bowl and gently slip the egg into the water. Repeat with the remaining eggs. (If you are poaching two eggs for each serving, cook the eggs in two batches.) Simmer until the whites are firm and the yolks are still slightly runny, about 4 minutes. Using a slotted spoon, lift out each egg, first blotting the bottom on the towel-lined plate and then transferring the egg to the large plate.

To assemble and serve, using a spoon, dollop the herbed garlic yogurt onto four plates, dividing it evenly. Using the back of the spoon, spread the yogurt in a circle, dragging the spoon through it to create ridges. Top each yogurt circle with an egg (or two). Spoon the chile butter over the eggs and yogurt. Mound the herb salad alongside, dividing it evenly. Sprinkle everything with a little salt and serve with the pita.

Nutrition Values (per serving): Energy (kJ) ~1760 kJ, Calories ~420 kcal, Fat ~28 g, Saturated Fat ~14 g, Carbohydrate ~18 g, Sugar ~4 g, Dietary Fiber ~2 g, Protein ~18 g, Cholesterol ~220 mg, Sodium ~480 mg

MAKES 4 SERVINGS

HERBED GARLIC YOGURT

1¼ cups (300 g) plain Greek yogurt

1 large garlic clove, finely grated

2 Tbsp finely chopped fresh dill

Kosher salt and freshly ground black pepper

SMOKY CHILE BUTTER

4 Tbsp (55 g) unsalted butter

2 tsp Aleppo pepper flakes

½ tsp smoked paprika

¼ tsp ground cumin

Pinch of kosher salt

HERB SALAD

2 Persian cucumbers, thinly sliced

1 cup chopped butter lettuce

2 Tbsp chopped fresh dill

2 Tbsp chopped fresh parsley

Extra virgin olive oil, for drizzling

Juice of ½ lemon

Pinch of kosher salt

POACHED EGGS

1 Tbsp distilled white vinegar

4 to 8 large eggs

Warm pita or flatbread, for serving

Beet-Quinoa Veggie Burgers with Pickled Onions & Avocado

Even if you think you don't like beets, you'll find these veggie burgers irresistible. Their jewel-toned purple hue hints at all the wholesome ingredients they contain, yet they are also pure comfort food. The patties freeze beautifully, so you can save some for another meal. Or you can double them up and serve four towering "double double" burgers that will wow everyone at the table.

MAKES 8 BURGERS

¼ cup (45 g) quinoa, rinsed under cold running water

½ cup (120 ml) water

Kosher salt and freshly ground pepper

1 medium red beet, trimmed, peeled, and finely shredded (about 1 cup/140 g total)

1 (15-oz/430-g) can black beans, drained and rinsed

½ cup (20 g) fresh breadcrumbs

1 large egg

¼ cup (35 g) minced yellow onion

1 Tbsp Dijon mustard

½ tsp smoked paprika

½ tsp cumin

Vegetable oil, for cooking

8 burger buns, split and toasted

Mayonnaise and/or country Dijon mustard, for serving

½ cup (60 g) pickled onions, homemade (page 79) or store-bought

1 large ripe avocado, halved, pitted, peeled, and thinly sliced

8 butter lettuce leaves

To cook the quinoa, in a small saucepan, combine the quinoa, water, and a pinch of salt and bring to a boil over high heat, stirring once or twice. Turn down the heat to low, cover, and cook until tender and the water has been completely absorbed, about 15 minutes. Remove from the heat and let cool. You should have ¾ cup (140 g).

Place the shredded beet in a fine-mesh sieve in the sink and squeeze and press out as much liquid as possible. Set aside.

To make the patties, put the beans into a food processor and pulse, stopping and scraping down the sides of the bowl as needed, until a rough mash forms. Add the beet, quinoa, breadcrumbs, egg, onion, mustard, paprika, cumin, ½ tsp salt, and ¼ tsp pepper and pulse, stopping to scrape down the sides of the bowl as needed, until mixed.

To form the patties, cut out eight 4½-inch (11.5-cm) squares of parchment paper. Scoop up the mixture into eight equal portions and mound each portion on a piece of parchment. Press each mound into a patty about ½ inch (12 mm) thick. Set aside. (The patties can be wrapped and frozen for up to 1 month.)

To cook the patties, heat a large, heavy nonstick skillet over medium-low heat. Add a drizzle of oil, then add the patties in a single layer. (You may need to do this in batches.) Cook, turning once or twice, until well browned and crisp on both sides and heated through, about 8 minutes.

To serve, spread each bun with mayonnaise and/or mustard. Place a patty on each bun bottom and top with pickled onions, avocado slices, and a lettuce leaf, then close with the bun top. Serve warm.

Nutrition Values (per burger): Energy (kJ) ~1510 kJ, Calories ~360 kcal, Fat ~14 g, Saturated Fat ~2 g, Carbohydrate ~46 g, Sugar ~6 g, Dietary Fiber ~8 g, Protein ~12 g, Cholesterol ~25 mg, Sodium ~620 mg

Sweet Treats 8

“Life can be unpredictable. Have dessert.”

–Michelle

No meal, no gathering, and certainly no cookbook is complete without a sweet finale. This is where the kitchen transforms into a joyful lab of sugar, butter, and happy sighs. This chapter is dedicated to those perfect indulgences that bring a little extra sparkle to life.

For fifteen years, I immersed myself in the art of pastry, both as a chef and while teaching at the esteemed French Culinary Institute. That experience taught me that the best desserts are those that balance precise technique with genuine warmth. The recipes in this collection embody that philosophy: reliable, delicious, and designed to bring that high-level satisfaction into your home kitchen.

Both classics and new favorites are celebrated in these pages. You will discover such handheld treasures as delicate Biscochitos and rich Double Chocolate Banana Muffins and such beautiful fruit desserts as Apple Crumble Tart and Blueberry-Lemon Skillet Cake. For chocolate lovers, the Chocolate Brownie Cookies are a must-try. And for sharing, the flaky Chocolate Pistachio Baklava Bites and the nostalgic Apple Cider Doughnut Bread Pudding are perfect.

These aren't just recipes. They are invitations to pause, celebrate, and connect over a treat made with love and a touch of professional wisdom. Let the sweet adventure begin!

—Michelle

Chocolate Brownie Cookies

These cookies hit the perfect balance between delicate and indulgent. Fudgy centers with just the right amount of chew meet a crackly, slightly crisp exterior, and rich cocoa powder, a hint of espresso powder, and chunks of bittersweet chocolate deliver deep, complex flavor. Easy to mix and bake, they offer all the satisfaction of a classic brownie in an easy-to-grab cookie.

MAKES ABOUT 22 COOKIES

1 cup (140 g) all-purpose flour

½ cup (40 g) Dutch-process cocoa powder

1 tsp instant espresso powder

½ tsp baking powder

½ tsp kosher salt

6 Tbsp (85 g) unsalted butter

4 oz (115 g) bittersweet chocolate, chopped

1¼ cups (250 g) sugar

3 large eggs

1 tsp vanilla extract

½ cup (90 g) mini or regular semisweet chocolate chips

Position two oven racks in the middle of the oven and preheat the oven to 325°F (165°C). Line two sheet pans with parchment paper or silicone baking mats.

To make the dough, in a medium bowl, whisk together the flour, cocoa powder, espresso powder, baking powder, and salt. In a medium saucepan over low heat, melt the butter. Add the chopped chocolate and stir gently with the whisk just until melted. Whisk in the sugar until well blended. The mixture will look grainy. Remove from the heat and whisk in the eggs and vanilla, mixing well. Add the flour mixture to the saucepan and, using a rubber spatula, stir just until blended. Stir in the chocolate chips.

Using a 2-Tbsp cookie scoop, scoop eight mounds of dough onto each prepared baking sheet, spacing them about 2 inches (5 cm) apart. (You will need to bake these cookies in two batches.)

Bake the cookies, switching the pans between the racks about halfway through baking, until slightly puffed and cooked through but shiny, about 11 minutes. As soon as you pull the pans out of the oven, bang them each once on the countertop. Let the cookies cool on the pans on wire racks for about 5 minutes, then transfer the cookies to the racks to cool completely before serving. Let a sheet pan cool for a few minutes, then shape the remaining dough and bake the cookies the same way. Leftover cookies will keep in an airtight container at room temperature for up to 1 week.

Nutrition Values (per cookie): Energy (kJ) ~950 kJ, Calories ~225 kcal, Fat ~9 g, Saturated Fat ~5 g, Carbohydrate ~33 g, Sugar ~24g, Dietary Fiber ~2 g, Protein ~3 g, Cholesterol ~35 mg, Sodium ~90 mg

Biscochitos

Biscochitos, the official cookie of New Mexico, appear all over the state during the holidays—and for Sustainability Team member Katie Garcia Homa, they're a cherished family tradition. Made by the women in her family for more than five generations, these cookies get their tender texture from lard and their heady flavor from a splash of brandy and a hint of anise. Rolled, cut, and dipped in cinnamon sugar (the kids' favorite job!), they're sublime with coffee or Mexican hot cocoa.

MAKES ABOUT 24 COOKIES

3 cups (420 g) all-purpose flour

1½ tsp baking powder

½ tsp kosher salt

1 cup (225 g) lard, at room temperature

1 cup (200 g) sugar

1 Tbsp aniseeds

1 large egg, beaten

¼ cup (60 ml) brandy or whiskey

1 tsp ground cinnamon

To make the dough, in a medium bowl, sift together the flour, baking powder, and salt. In a stand mixer fitted with the paddle attachment, beat together the lard, ¾ cup (150 g) of the sugar, and the aniseeds on medium speed, stopping to scrape down the sides of the bowl as needed, until light and fluffy, about 3 minutes. Add the egg and brandy and beat until well blended, then beat in the dry ingredients

On low speed, add the flour mixture in two or three additions, beating just until blended after each addition. The dough will be stiff. Remove the bowl from the mixer stand, cover, and refrigerate the dough until chilled, at least 30 minutes or up to 1 day.

Position two oven racks in the middle of the oven and preheat the oven to 350°F (175°C). Line two sheet pans with parchment paper or silicone baking mats.

To roll and cut the dough, transfer it to a lightly floured work surface and shape into a thick disk. Roll out the dough ¼ inch (6 mm) thick. Using a bench scraper or a large knife, cut the dough into diamond shapes about 3 inches (7.5 cm) tall and 2 inches (5 cm) wide.

In a wide, shallow small bowl, stir together the remaining ¼ cup (50 g) sugar and the cinnamon. One at a time, press the top of each dough diamond into the cinnamon-sugar mixture, then transfer, cinnamon sugar–side up, to the prepared sheet pans.

Bake the cookies, switching the pans between the racks about halfway through baking, until lightly browned, 12 to 15 minutes. Let cool on the pans on wire racks for 5 minutes, then transfer the cookies to the racks to cool completely before serving.

Nutrition Values (per cookie): Energy (kJ) ~810 kJ, Calories ~195 kcal, Fat ~10 g, Saturated Fat ~4 g, Carbohydrate ~23 g, Sugar ~11 g, Dietary Fiber ~0 g, Protein ~2 g, Cholesterol ~16 mg, Sodium ~9 mg

Kamish Bread

Kamish bread—also known as mandel bread or mandelbrot—is a cherished family recipe for Procurement Market team member Rebecca Bordelon. Made with her grandmother whenever Rebecca and her family visited, these twice-baked cookies are crafted with love and freeze beautifully, making them ideal for sharing. Sweet and nutty, they carry the nostalgia of family kitchens and holidays, with each bite offering a connection to tradition and the warmth of home.

MAKES ABOUT 3 DOZEN COOKIES

About 3½ cups (490 g) all-purpose flour

1½ cups (300 g) sugar

1 tsp baking powder

1 tsp ground cinnamon

¼ tsp kosher salt

3 large eggs

1⅓ cups (315 ml) vegetable oil

1 tsp vanilla extract

½ tsp fresh lemon juice

½ cup (60 g) chopped toasted pecans or walnuts

½ cup (70 g) raisins

CINNAMON SUGAR

¼ cup (50 g) sugar

1 tsp ground cinnamon

To make the dough, in a large bowl, whisk together 3 cups (420 g) of the flour, the sugar, baking powder, cinnamon, and salt. In another bowl, whisk together the eggs, oil, vanilla, and lemon juice, mixing well. Add the egg mixture to the flour mixture and stir until combined. Fold in the pecans and raisins. Gradually stir in as much of the remaining ½ cup (70 g) flour as needed to form a stiff, sticky dough.

Preheat the oven to 375°F (190°C). Lightly spray a large sheet pan with cooking spray.

To shape the dough, using floured hands, divide the dough in half. Transfer half of the dough to the prepared sheet pan. Shape the dough into a log about 1 inch (2.5 cm) wide and 14 inches (36 cm) long, positioning it lengthwise on half of the pan. Shape the remaining dough half the same way, positioning it on the other half of the pan and spacing the logs about 2 inches (5 cm) apart.

To make the cinnamon sugar, in a bowl, stir together the sugar and cinnamon, mixing well. Sprinkle half of the cinnamon sugar on the tops of the logs, dividing it evenly.

Bake the logs for 15 minutes, then remove the pan from the oven and transfer the logs to a cutting board. Using a large serrated knife, cut each log crosswise on the diagonal into slices ¾ inch (2 cm) thick. Return the slices to the baking sheet cut-side down, spacing them slightly apart. Sprinkle evenly with the remaining cinnamon sugar.

Return the cookies to the oven and bake until crisp and golden brown, 10 to 12 minutes. Let cool for 5 minutes, then transfer to a wire rack to cool completely. Leftover cookies will keep for up to 1 week.

Nutrition Values (per cookie): Energy (kJ) ~746 kJ, Calories ~178 kcal, Fat ~9 g, Saturated Fat ~1 g, Carbohydrate ~21 g, Sugar ~12 g, Dietary Fiber ~1 g, Protein ~2 g, Cholesterol ~16 mg, Sodium ~15 mg

Apple Crumble Tart

A buttery, flaky crust, spiced apple filling, and crisp, sweet crumble topping make up this showy autumn dessert that's both homespun and elegant. While homemade dough takes it over the top, a frozen all-butter crust works when you're pressed for time. You can even make the components ahead of time, so when it's tart day, assembly—and the wow factor—is a breeze.

MAKES 6 TO 8 SERVINGS

DOUGH

1 large egg yolk

2 Tbsp cold water

1 tsp vanilla extract

1¼ cups (175 g) all-purpose flour

2 Tbsp granulated sugar

¼ tsp kosher salt

½ cup (110 g) cold unsalted butter, cut into ¾-inch (2-cm) cubes

CRUMBLE TOPPING

1 cup (140 g) all-purpose flour

⅓ cup (65 g) granulated sugar

¼ tsp kosher salt

5 Tbsp (70 g) unsalted butter, melted and cooled

1 tsp vanilla extract

APPLE FILLING

1 Tbsp unsalted butter

2 lb (900 g) crisp-tart baking apples, such as Granny Smith or Honeycrisp, peeled, halved, cored, and cut into slices ¼ inch (6 mm) thick

Juice of ½ lemon

½ cup (100 g) packed light brown sugar

¼ cup (50 g) granulated sugar

1 Tbsp all-purpose flour

¼ tsp ground cinnamon

To make the dough, in a small bowl, whisk together the egg yolk, water, and vanilla. In a food processor, combine the flour, granulated sugar, and salt and pulse two or three times to mix. Scatter the butter over the flour mixture and pulse until the butter is the size of peas and the mixture looks like large breadcrumbs. Pour the egg mixture into the flour mixture and pulse until the mixture is evenly moistened and starts to clump. It will still be crumbly.

Dump the dough onto a work surface and press into a flat disk. Wrap tightly in plastic wrap (or put it into an airtight container) and refrigerate for at least 30 minutes or up to overnight. (The dough can be frozen for up to 1 month. Thaw overnight in the refrigerator.)

To line the tart pan, lightly spray a 9½- or 10-inch (24- or 25-cm) tart pan with a removable bottom with cooking spray. On a lightly floured work surface, roll out the dough into a round about ⅛ inch (3 mm) thick and 12 to 13 inches (30 to 33 cm) in diameter. If the dough tears, just press it back together.

Carefully transfer the round to the prepared tart pan, centering it and then gently easing it into the bottom and up the sides of the pan. Trim the dough, leaving a 1-inch (2.5-cm) overhang. Fold the dough back onto itself down the inside of the pan and press together to create a reinforced rim. Freeze for at least 15 minutes or up to 1 week.

To make the crumble topping, in a bowl, using a fork, stir together the flour, granulated sugar, and salt. Add the butter and vanilla and stir until evenly blended and crumbly. Use right away or cover and refrigerate for up to overnight. (If refrigerated, remove from the refrigerator before rolling the dough so the topping can soften slightly.)

continued . . .

Apple Crumble Tart

continued from page 235 . . .

To make the filling, in a large skillet over medium heat, melt the butter. Add the apple slices, lemon juice, both sugars, the flour, and cinnamon and cook, stirring, until the apples are tender-crisp and the juices are thick and syrupy, about 8 minutes. Remove from the heat and let cool completely.

Preheat the oven to 375°F (190°C).

To assemble and bake the tart, place the tart pan on a sheet pan. Using a slotted spoon, spoon the cooled filling into the chilled tart shell. If the filling is very juicy, only add enough of the juices that will fit in the pan with the apples. Top with the crumble topping, spreading it in an even layer.

Bake the tart until the filling is bubbly and the crumble and crust are golden brown, about 55 minutes. Let cool in the pan on a wire rack for at least 30 minutes before serving.

To unmold and serve, place the tart pan on an overturned bowl slightly smaller than the pan base and push down gently on the pan rim, releasing it downward. Carefully slide a wide offset spatula between the pan base and the crust and transfer the tart to a serving plate. The tart can be served warm, at room temperature, or chilled. Cut into wedges to serve.

Cook's Notes

Swap in the same amount of ripe pears (peeled, cored, and chopped) for the apples and add ¼ cup (25 g) sliced almonds to the crumble topping. Depending on the ripeness of the pears, they may be juicier and not take as long to cook, so adjust the amount of flour and cook time as needed.

Nutrition Values (per serving for 8 servings): Energy (kJ) ~1760 kJ, Calories ~410 kcal, Fat ~20 g, Saturated Fat ~14 g, Carbohydrate ~49 g, Sugar ~28 g, Dietary Fiber ~4 g, Protein ~4 g, Cholesterol ~85 mg, Sodium ~155 mg

Strawberry Cheesecake Puffs

Reminiscent of a quick cheese Danish—without the fuss of making dough from scratch—these puffs are filled with a cheesecake-like cream cheese mixture and a dollop of fruity jam. Buttery and tender, this dessert can also star at breakfast or teatime. A simple glaze adds a lovely touch.

MAKES 8 PUFFS

PUFFS

1 (17- to 18-oz/485- to 505-g) package puff pastry (2 sheets), thawed in the refrigerator

1 (8-oz/225-g) package cream cheese, at room temperature

¼ cup (50 g) granulated sugar

1 large egg, separated

1 tsp fresh lemon juice

1 tsp vanilla extract

2 tsp water

⅓ cup (100 g) strawberry or other berry jam

GLAZE (OPTIONAL)

⅓ cup (40 g) powdered sugar

2 tsp whole milk

To make the puff pastry bases, line two sheet pans with parchment paper or silicone baking mats. On a lightly floured work surface, roll out each pastry sheet into a rectangle about 9 by 12 inches (23 by 30 cm). Cut each sheet into four 4½-by-6-inch (11.5-by-15-cm) rectangles. Transfer four pastry rectangles to each prepared sheet pan, spacing them apart. Using a paring knife, score the edge of each pastry rectangle, leaving a ½-inch (12-mm) border and being careful not to cut all the way through. Using a fork, prick the middle of each rectangle a few times. Refrigerate the puff pastry for 15 to 30 minutes.

Position two oven racks in the middle of the oven and preheat the oven to 375°F (190°C).

To make the cheesecake mixture, in a bowl, using a handheld mixer, beat together the cream cheese and granulated sugar on medium speed until smooth and fluffy, about 1 minute. Add the egg yolk, lemon juice, and vanilla and beat until very smooth and silky, about 3 minutes, stopping to scrape down the sides of the bowl as needed.

To assemble the puffs, in a bowl, whisk together the egg white and water until frothy. Dollop the cheesecake mixture onto the center of each pastry rectangle, dividing it evenly. Spread it in an even layer up to the scored border. Dollop about 2 tsp jam onto the cheesecake mixture, then use a knife tip, swirl in the jam. Using a pastry brush, brush the border of each pastry base lightly with the egg white mixture.

Bake the pastries, switching the pans between the racks halfway through baking, until puffed, crisp, and golden brown, about 30 minutes. Let cool on the pans on wire racks for 30 minutes.

To make the glaze, whisk together the powdered sugar and milk. Drizzle the glaze over the cooled pastries. Let set, then serve.

Nutrition Values (per puff): Energy (kJ) ~1340 kJ, Calories ~320 kcal, Fat ~20 g, Saturated Fat ~10 g, Carbohydrate ~30 g, Sugar ~12 g, Dietary Fiber ~1 g, Protein ~4 g, Cholesterol ~45 mg, Sodium ~220 mg

Blueberry-Lemon Skillet Cake

Baked in an ovenproof skillet, this blueberry-lemon cake can be enjoyed as dessert with a scoop of vanilla ice cream or plain as a snacking cake with a cup of tea. Bursting with juicy blueberries and fragrant lemon zest, it has a soft, buttery crumb and a subtle sugary top. Try it with other berries, too, such as raspberries or blackberries.

MAKES 8 SERVINGS

1½ cups (210 g) all-purpose flour

2 tsp baking powder

½ tsp baking soda

½ tsp kosher salt

½ cup (110 g) unsalted butter, at room temperature

1 cup (200 g) plus 2 Tbsp sugar

Finely grated zest of 2 lemons

2 large eggs

1 tsp vanilla extract

½ cup sour cream

2 Tbsp fresh lemon juice

2 cups (280 g) fresh blueberries

Vanilla ice cream or whipped cream, for serving (optional)

Preheat the oven to 350°F (175°C). Spray a 10-inch (25-cm) ovenproof skillet with cooking spray.

To make the batter, in a medium bowl, whisk together the flour, baking powder, baking soda, and salt. In large bowl, using a handheld mixer, beat together the butter, 1 cup (200 g) of the sugar, and the lemon zest on medium speed until well mixed, about 3 minutes. Add the eggs, one at a time, beating after each addition until blended. On low speed, add the vanilla and beat until blended. Stop the mixer and scrape down the sides of the bowl with a rubber spatula.

On low speed, add half of the flour mixture and beat just until blended. Add the sour cream and lemon juice and beat just until incorporated, then beat in the remaining flour mixture until combined. Using the rubber spatula, stir in the blueberries.

To bake the cake, pour the batter into the prepared skillet and spread in an even layer. Sprinkle the remaining 2 Tbsp sugar evenly over the top. Bake until golden brown and a toothpick inserted into the center of the cake comes out clean, about 45 minutes. Let cool completely in the skillet on a wire rack.

To serve, cut into wedges and accompany each serving with a scoop of ice cream, if desired.

Nutrition Values (per serving): Energy (kJ) ~1295 kJ, Calories ~310 kcal, Fat ~14 g, Saturated Fat ~8 g, Carbohydrate ~42 g, Sugar ~24 g, Dietary Fiber ~2 g, Protein ~4 g, Cholesterol ~65 mg, Sodium ~220 mg

Sour Cherry Jam Bars

These jam bars are delightfully simple and endlessly adaptable. The tart-sweet flavor of sour cherry jam evokes classic cherry pie, but you can swap in nearly any jam you like, such as strawberry, peach, or mixed berry. A tender, buttery base with just a touch of cinnamon holds the jam perfectly. Easy to make and portable, these bars are ideal for tucking into lunch boxes or packing for a road trip.

MAKES 8 BARS

1 large egg yolk

1 Tbsp whole milk

1 tsp vanilla extract

1⅓ cups (185 g) all-purpose flour

½ cup (100 g) sugar

½ tsp baking powder

½ tsp kosher salt

¼ tsp ground cinnamon

½ cup (110 g) unsalted butter, cut into chunks, at room temperature

1 cup (300 g) sour cherry jam or your favorite jam flavor

Preheat the oven to 375°F (190°C). Lightly butter the bottom and sides of an 8-inch (20-cm) square baking pan, then line the bottom and two sides with parchment paper, leaving a slight overhang over the sides.

To make the dough, in a small bowl, whisk together the egg yolk, milk, and vanilla. In a food processor, combine the flour, sugar, baking powder, salt, and cinnamon and pulse two or three times to mix. Scatter the butter over the flour mixture and pulse until the mixture looks like large breadcrumbs. Pour the egg mixture into the flour mixture and pulse until the mixture is evenly moistened and starts to clump. It will still be crumbly.

To assemble and bake the bars, pour about three-fourths of the dough into the bottom of the prepared baking pan. Spread it in an even layer and then press it firmly into the pan (the flat bottom of a glass works well for this). Spread the jam on top in an even layer. Crumble the remaining dough mixture evenly over the jam.

Bake until the top and sides are golden brown, about 30 minutes. Let cool completely in the pan, then cut into eight bars and serve. Leftover bars will keep in an airtight container at room temperature for up to 1 week.

Nutrition Values (per bar): Energy (kJ) ~1090 kJ, Calories ~260 kcal, Fat ~12 g, Saturated Fat ~7 g, Carbohydrate ~34 g, Sugar ~18 g, Dietary Fiber ~1 g, Protein ~3 g, Cholesterol ~45 mg, Sodium ~120 mg

Chocolate Pistachio Baklava Bites

These bites put a playful twist on the classic Middle Eastern dessert. Rolled like a cinnamon roll and baked cut-side up, they reveal a distinctive swirl of buttery filo layered with roasted pistachios, chocolate, and cinnamon. They are finished with a generous drizzle of honey syrup and chocolate, making each piece crisp, nutty, and decadently sweet. Don't skimp on the syrup. It keeps the baklava perfectly soaked. For the best results, use a pan that holds the bites snugly or wedge in a piece of foil to keep them secure.

MAKES 12 PIECES

BAKLAVA

4 oz (115 g) unsalted roasted pistachios

½ cup (90 g) semisweet chocolate chips

¼ cup (50 g) sugar

½ tsp ground cinnamon

Pinch of kosher salt

About 6 Tbsp (85 g) unsalted butter, melted

9 (14-by-9-inch/36-by-23-cm) sheets frozen filo dough, thawed in the refrigerator according to package directions

HONEY SYRUP

⅓ cup (65 g) sugar

¼ cup (85 g) honey

¼ cup (60 ml) water

1 cinnamon stick

1 orange peel strip

GARNISH

¼ cup (45 g) semisweet chocolate chips, melted

2 Tbsp finely chopped unsalted roasted pistachios

Preheat the oven to 350°F (175°F).

To make the filling, in a food processor, combine the pistachios, chocolate chips, sugar, cinnamon, and salt and pulse until the mixture is roughly ground. Do not process them into a fine meal. Divide the mixture evenly among three small bowls.

Brush the bottom and sides of an 8-inch (20-cm) square baking dish with melted butter.

To layer the filo, unroll the thawed filo sheets and cover with a damp kitchen towel to prevent drying. Lay one filo sheet on a clean work surface with the long side facing you. Brush the top lightly with melted butter. Add a second filo sheet and brush with butter. Top with a third filo sheet and brush with butter. Pour the pistachio filling from one small bowl onto the filo stack and spread evenly over the top.

Lay a filo sheet on top of the pistachio mixture and brush lightly with butter. Repeat with a second sheet and butter and then a third sheet and butter. Pour the pistachio filling from a second small bowl onto the filo stack and spread evenly over the top. Repeat to add three more filo sheets, brushing each with butter. Spread the final bowl of the pistachio mixture evenly over the top.

To roll the baklava, starting from the long edge farthest from you, tightly roll the layered filo toward you, brushing the log with melted butter as needed to make sure the layers stick together. With the log seam-side down, and using a sharp knife, cut the log crosswise into twelve rolls each about 1 inch (2.5 cm) wide. Transfer the rolls cut-side up to the prepared baking dish. They should fit snugly together. If they don't, fill the empty space with a wadded-up piece of aluminum foil.

continued . . .

Chocolate Pistachio Baklava Bites

continued from page 242 . . .

Bake the rolls for 30 minutes, then cover the pan with aluminum foil and continue to bake until crisp and golden brown, about 30 minutes longer.

Make the syrup while the baklava bakes. In a saucepan, stir together the sugar, honey, water, cinnamon stick, and orange peel. Bring to a boil over medium-high heat, stirring to dissolve the sugar and honey, then turn down the heat to low and simmer, stirring occasionally, until a slightly syrupy consistency forms, about 15 minutes. Remove from the heat and let cool to room temperature.

When the baklava is done, transfer the baking dish to a wire rack. Remove the cinnamon stick and orange peel from the syrup and discard. Slowly pour the syrup evenly over the baklava. Set aside at room temperature for at least 4 hours or up to overnight before garnishing and serving.

To garnish and serve, drizzle the baklava with the melted chocolate and sprinkle with the pistachios. Let sit for a few minutes to set the chocolate, then serve. The baklava can be stored in an airtight container at room temperature or in the refrigerator for up to 2 weeks.

Nutrition Values (per piece): Energy (kJ) ~1090 kJ, Calories ~260 kcal, Fat ~16 g, Saturated Fat ~7 g, Carbohydrate ~28 g, Sugar ~14 g, Dietary Fiber ~2 g, Protein ~4 g, Cholesterol ~20 mg, Sodium ~80 mg

Double Chocolate Banana Muffins

After being diagnosed with eosinophilic esophagitis, Product Strategy team member Stephanie Ulrich had to rethink her diet entirely. In the process, she discovered the joy of cooking and created allergy-friendly recipes to share with others facing similar challenges. Her Double Chocolate Banana Muffins, made with tigernut flour and arrowroot powder (a.k.a. arrowroot flour or starch), are vegan, grain-free, and nut-free—yet rich, decadent, and delicious. Tigernut flour, a naturally sweet, nutrient-packed root-vegetable powder, provides fiber, prebiotics, and a subtly nutty flavor. It can be difficult to source, however, but cassava flour or almond flour makes a good substitute.

MAKES 6 MUFFINS

- 1 Tbsp chia seeds
- 3 Tbsp water
- 1 cup (120 g) tigernut flour (see note above)
- ½ cup (60 g) arrowroot powder
- ⅓ cup (25 g) natural cocoa powder
- 1 tsp baking soda
- ½ tsp kosher salt
- 1 ripe banana, peeled and mashed (about ½ cup/115 g)
- ½ cup (120 ml) avocado oil
- ¼ cup (60 ml) maple syrup
- 1 tsp vanilla extract
- ½ cup (90 g) semisweet or bittersweet chocolate chips, plus more for sprinkling
- 2 Tbsp apple cider vinegar

Preheat the oven to 350°F (175°C). Line six standard muffin cups with paper liners.

To prepare the chia seed egg, in a small bowl, whisk together the chia seeds and water, then set aside to thicken for at least 5 minutes.

To make the batter, in a medium bowl, whisk together the tigernut flour, arrowroot powder, cocoa powder, baking soda, and salt. In a second medium bowl, stir together the banana, oil, maple syrup, and vanilla. Add the flour mixture to the banana mixture and stir to mix. Fold in the chocolate chips. Finally, fold in the chia seed egg, then stir in the vinegar. Do not overmix.

Divide the batter evenly among the lined muffin cups. Sprinkle the top of each filled cup with a few chocolate chips.

Bake the muffins until puffed and a toothpick inserted into the center of a muffin comes out clean, 20 to 23 minutes. Let the muffins cool in the pan on a wire rack for 15 minutes, then transfer the muffins to the wire rack to cool and set completely before serving.

Nutrition Values (per muffin): Energy (kJ) ~1775 kJ, Calories ~424 kcal, Fat ~28 g, Saturated Fat ~6 g, Carbohydrate ~45 g, Sugar ~20 g, Dietary Fiber ~10 g, Protein ~3 g, Cholesterol 0 mg, Sodium ~64 mg

Apple Cider Doughnut Bread Pudding

This recipe reminds Culinary Team member Courtney Roker Laga of crisp October days in the Berkshires. After a morning spent picking apples at a local orchard, her family would always treat themselves to freshly made apple cider doughnuts—usually more than they could eat. A day or two later, any leftover doughnuts found new life in this cozy bread pudding, turning slightly stale sweets into a memorable fall dessert.

MAKES 6 SERVINGS

3 large eggs

2 cups (475 ml) heavy cream

1 cup (240 ml) whole milk

½ cup (100 g) granulated sugar

½ tsp ground cinnamon

½ tsp vanilla extract

10 stale apple cider doughnuts, torn into 2-inch (5-cm) pieces

¼ cup (50 g) packed light brown sugar

Preheat the oven to 350°F (175°C). Spray an 8-inch (20-cm) square baking pan with cooking spray.

To make the custard, in a medium bowl, whisk together the eggs, cream, milk, granulated sugar, cinnamon, and vanilla until well blended.

To assemble the pudding, arrange the doughnut cubes in an even layer in the bottom of the prepared pan. Pour the custard mixture evenly over the doughnuts, then press down on the doughnuts so they soak up the custard base. Sprinkle the brown sugar evenly over the top.

To bake the pudding, cover the pan with aluminum foil and bake until nearly set, 20 to 25 minutes. Remove the foil and continue to bake until the filling is set and no longer jiggles when the pan is shaken and the top is golden brown, about 15 minutes longer. Transfer the pan to a wire rack to cool slightly before serving.

Serve the pudding warm or at room temperature.

Nutrition Values (per serving): Energy (kJ) ~2175 kJ, Calories ~520 kcal, Fat ~32 g, Saturated Fat ~18 g, Carbohydrate ~52 g, Sugar ~30 g, Dietary Fiber ~1 g, Protein ~7 g, Cholesterol ~165 mg, Sodium ~220 mg

INDEX

M

N

O

P

Q

R

S

T

U

V

W

Y

Z

Acknowledgments

This book is the product of many hands, many hearts, and a shared belief that cooking fresh food at home can bring people closer together. We are deeply grateful to everyone who contributed to creating *HelloFresh Unboxed*.

First and foremost, we want to thank the incredible HelloFresh Test Kitchen and Culinary Team—Avram Salzman, Christina Boateng, Courtney Laga Roker, Daniel Kim, Jay Chan, Marina Schulze, Oliver Meder, and Sara Heilman—the chefs, recipe developers, testers, and culinary managers who bring creativity, rigor, and care to every recipe. Your energy, curiosity, and commitment to excellence are the foundation of this book and of the meals enjoyed by millions of households every week.

We are especially grateful to Adam Kalikow for his support of this project and his belief in celebrating the people and process behind the box. Thank you for championing a book that showcases the craft, culture, and creativity of the HelloFresh family.

A heartfelt thank you to Ana Garcia, Jeffrey Yorzyk, and our sustainability team for bringing Meals with Meaning to life. It reflects the very spirit of this cookbook: using food to care for and connect communities.

We also extend our thanks to Colavita and Roland Foods, trusted partners whose exceptional olive oils and pantry staples reflect the standards we believe in: quality ingredients, thoughtful sourcing, and respect for tradition.

Thank you to our customers, friends, and families. You inspire everything we cook. Your feedback, your stories, and the meals you make at home guide us every day. This book is for you and because of you.

We are grateful to Salty Days Media, whose vision and collaboration made this cookbook possible. Thank you to Publisher and CEO Sara Domville for her belief in this project and her unwavering enthusiasm for bringing brand stories to life through food. Our deepest thanks to Editorial Director Kim Laidlaw, whose leadership, insight, and care shaped the manuscript with clarity and heart, and to Creative Director Ali Zeigler, whose artistic vision brought warmth, modernity, and beauty to every page.

We are also thankful for the entire Salty Days Dream Team, including photographer Michael Piazza, whose images capture food with honesty and soul, and Joy Howard, Rachel Michel, and Laura Sui, whose styling and behind-the-scenes work elevated every recipe.

Special thanks to Josh Olken for his support of our entire culinary innovation team during this project. We were also graciously assisted by the HelloFresh communications team of Abigail Dreher, Victoria Musso, and Robyn Schweitzer, who provided guidance and support throughout production. Finally, we are indebted to our recipe testers and specialists, Kim Laidlaw, Frank Lorenzoni, Olivia Miller, Shirley Fairclough, Gretchen Grant, and the Trani family, whose feedback, along with that of our friends and family, was essential in refining these recipes for the home cook.

KRISTIN BRYAN

MICHELLE DOLL OLSON

KRISTIN BRYAN is the head of US Culinary Innovation at HelloFresh. A professional chef, business leader, founder, and author, Kristin blends creativity and strategy to design food experiences that spark curiosity, elevate everyday cooking, and bring people together around the table. With more than two decades in product innovation, food design, and content development, Kristin leads the culinary teams responsible for shaping what millions of home cooks experience in their kitchens each week. Before joining HelloFresh, Kristin served on the culinary team at an award-winning restaurant at Walt Disney World, co-founded the culinary storytelling platform The Chef Sisters, and worked as a leadership architect, developing teams, processes, and creative cultures that drive lasting impact.

MICHELLE DOLL OLSON, senior culinary development manager at HelloFresh, leads a team of talented recipe developers, overseeing the creation of thousands of recipes for millions of home cooks. A graduate of the French Culinary Institute, Michelle is a professional chef, culinary educator, and author whose career has spanned New York City's pastry scene and global food trends, though she is perhaps best known for her culinary precision, a skill she displayed on Food Network's *Throwdown with Bobby Flay,* besting the Iron Chef. Michelle is the author of *Essential Tools, Tips & Techniques for the Home Cook,* teaches master classes on Craftsy, and regularly contributes to national publications.

MICHAEL PIAZZA is a food, portrait, and lifestyle photographer and director based in Boston, Massachusetts. Originally from California, Michael studied art history and film before moving to New York City, where he began shooting cookbooks early in his career. In addition to working as a freelance photographer and director, he is the chief photographer and creative director of *Edible Boston* magazine. Michael contributes to publications such as *Bon Appétit, Condé Nast Traveler, Food & Wine, Imbibe, Men's Health, The New York Times, Travel + Leisure, Wall Street Journal,* and *Yankee.*